WE ARE ALL ONE

A call to spiritual uprising

J.M. Harrison

Ego vox clamantis in deserto.
Hoc est testimonium Joannis.

We Are All One

Printed and Published by BookSurge

A Lawren O'Lee Publication.

Copyright © 2007 J.M. Harrison

All rights reserved.

ISBN: 1-4196-7405-6

ISBN-13: 9781419674051

Library of Congress Control Number: 2007905924

Cover artwork: Sharon Jeffries

Cover design: Lyn Bowler

Table of Contents

About This Book 1
Preface 7
Chapter One: CONSCIOUS EVOLVEMENT IN OUR TIME . 9
Chapter Two: SPATIAL CONSCIOUSNESS 29
Chapter Three: TRUTH IN OUR TIME 47
Chapter Four: THE PATH.. 53
Chapter Five: OURSELVES AND OTHERS 59
Chapter Six: PERCEPTION AND EXPERIENCE 69
Chapter Seven: SPATIAL QUALITIES AND THEIR USE ... 91
Chapter Eight: GOD OF OUR UNDERSTANDING 101
Chapter Nine: LOVELIGHT AND HEALING...................... 113
Chapter Ten: ASPECTS OF BEING....................................... 139
Chapter Eleven: REPROGRAMMING THROUGH SOUL
AND SPIRIT 151
Chapter Twelve: THE METASENSES 161
Summation... 179
Dubon 189

About This Book

Sitting down for an evening meal with my wife and some friends in the spring of 2002, the conversation turned towards the mystical; the déjà vu feeling, the reality of gut instinct and the sometimes seemingly bizarre occurrences that shape our lives and beliefs.

Suddenly, I was overcome by a sense of feeling strangely different. As the conversation continued, I entered what is called a trance state. Fortunately, one of our friends present that evening had seen this type of phenomenon before and explained encouragingly that what I was experiencing was a natural higher state of awareness. At this time I had no previous knowledge or particular interest in such matters. In fact in many ways I considered that I had a healthy, sceptical approach to the nature of the unknown.

What happened that night was to radically change my perspective of reality and understandings of the truths of existence. My senses were all heightened, I began to have visions, to talk in tongues and experience the altered states of trance mediumship and channeling. At one point in the evening, I was 'given' three insights into planet Earth; her past, present and future, but that's another story in itself.

Since these and further similar occurrences I have been actively seeking to comprehend the reality of my experiences. I have spent time attending courses run by some of the foremost spiritual teachers and healers available. On a personal level I have continued painstaking research of a wide variety of belief systems, sacred texts and philosophies, always striving to discern the perennial truths.

Giving up all 'business' interests and founding The 'Dubon' Center of Healing and Awareness in Gascony, France seemed a natural progression towards helping, healing and sharing with others on this incredible spiritual journey we call life. Through the setting up of 'Dubon' we have been continually blessed and have been further privileged that through our work, several 'new' or innovative types of healing have been brought to awareness.

All these experiences culminated in a life altering event that occurred early in 2007. One quiet evening at home, I 'received' a near death experience which was to change me for good. I remember collapsing on the floor and saying a simple 'Sorry' to apologise to my wife Wendy for any heartache or hurt that I had caused in the twenty-five years we had known each other. Then, I looked on as I was pulled up and out of the crown of my head to find myself gazing down at her. Beginning to understand what had actually happened, I remember thinking 'Maybe it's time for me to go…' After the initial shock, there was a peace, no struggle, no pain, just a feeling of acceptance. I began to accept that this could be 'it' and that my 'death' was imminent. As I looked down at Wendy, it was as if I was reading her thoughts. It became clear that both she and the children still needed me, that it was necessary to remain with them for the time being. Then, all of a sudden, I was drawn back into my body by what felt like a powerful 'magnetic' force. We stayed up late, both shaken by what had happened, discussing our personal experiences of what had occurred that evening. We talked well into the early hours knowing that something had changed.

The next day or two, still in shock, we rested as best we could. Then something strange happened. As the true reality of all that had happened sank in, my old process of thought was replaced by a new state of consciousness and I started to write. I didn't choose the words, the words chose me.

Some might say that what was written was 'channeled' material, but I would say that it was me becoming truly conscious. There was no need to explain the 'download' as coming from a being or group of beings, the physical or non-physical. I didn't want or need to be anything, had no preconceived plan or target, I just felt whole and complete.

I had blended with something that it is possible for everyone to connect with, the Source itself. Being 'plugged in' I could truly see and feel how everything was interconnected. Six days later, the book was complete.

Even today, with each reading I find something new hidden in the pages, for it is not just from me but from consciousness herself. The fullness of the message lies beyond the informational value of the words, making its true mystical presence known to those ready to receive it. This book is not about money and fame, or the 'secret' of how to get everything you want. If that is what you are looking for, then good luck to you, enjoy your journey. This book is about you revealing to yourself what you need, what you *really* need. So, if you are seeking to awaken yourself to the greatest potential that life can provide, then read on, for this book is about getting in contact with the best part of *you* and then utilizing that for the benefit of us *all*, because we are all One.

If you could have any 'thing' that you wanted, over time your requirements would change. You would eventually become bored with those material 'things' that you had previously desired and would want to replace them with others. But then one day you might want different 'things' altogether; the infinite things that are the true needs of your being.

My responsibility is to publish and share the truth and power contained in 'We Are All One' with the growing number of spiritual seekers in the world today.

I hope and pray that 'We Are All One' provides you with the inspiration you require at this point in your life and that it plays a role in your conscious evolution to a higher state of being, reawakening you to ***the incredible miracle that you are.***

JMH Dubon, France 2007.

Preface

Before we begin this book of mystery, some things need to be addressed.

There will be no 'I' found anywhere in these pages, there is no place for it, for spiritually speaking it does not exist.

This is a book of spiritual substance, not of intellect, opinion or judgement.

When we refer to spirit, we are pointing to the pervading divine essence at the heart of all existence.

The singling out of any individual being is done in order to provide examples of those pioneers who helped clear the way for the transformational process of spiritual evolution.

'We' is a collective expression that applies to us all, for

without each other, we would not exist.

The 'All' is a term for God. It describes the Great Spirit, the Source of All Being, the One, the essence of creation, and does in no way apply to any specific religion or belief, for if the truth existed in only one form, then the existence of God in all other systems of belief might be proven to be false and the God we are referring to is the One who exists in all forms, to all men, according to their understanding.

We may congratulate ourselves, knowing that we have come a long way on the evolutionary path and yet we constantly have to remind ourselves to push on and not to fall on the slippery rocks of the 'self.'

'We Are All One' is not a religion, or the result of one singular mind, but the result of all minds and the fruits of all religions, a compendium of past, present and future.

We are not separate entities. We are united. We are indivisible. For the truth of our spirit is this …

We Are All One.

Chapter One:
CONSCIOUS EVOLVEMENT IN OUR TIME

"We Are All One" enables an alignment of consciousness with our highest potential, not just the potential of the "you," the singular one, but of the "us," the all. It is an evolutionary transformational process redefining the concept of the ego-based "we," applying it not to an elite or separate group, but to everyone who exists, has existed or will exist. "We Are All One" is a state of consciousness that if put into practice will reveal the true nature of our selves to our individual "self," for it will bring out the spiritual essence, providing a system of understanding, release and expression.

The methodology does not require that you undertake decades of philosophical or intellectual study, or that you be especially gifted; neither does it require a large financial investment. It does not require membership to a secret society or adherence to a religion. No, all it requires is the initial willingness to understand that on the spiritual level we are all the same.

We can admit that we all look different from one another and come to terms with the fact that our minds can provide interesting doors to a wide variety of mental states, from madness to genius. But deep inside, really deep at the core of our being, we understand that we are the same and this causes us confusion, for the body seeks individuality in the form of appearance; and the mind seeks a stage from where to display its uniqueness and capacity, yet the spirit seeks unity with all, with itself.

This is the human dilemma, the mystery of mysteries since the beginning of time. We feel we are not just the body that we see and not purely the mind we utilize, that we are part of something much greater and there is nothing greater than our spiritual nature, because it is inclusive, it cannot exclude or discriminate, it is One and is indivisible.

When we feel disconnected from the whole (the Oneness), then we are in a **fractionate state**, so called because we are in denial or unconscious of being whole. This is a negative state of being and one that encourages further division to enter our lives. Situations arise in day to day life giving us the opportunity to allow or deny our alignment with this 'fractionation'. For example; if we become upset, do we hold onto that anger or do we choose to let it go by accepting and forgiving? If we see success and happiness in others are we envious and jealous or do we congratulate them, sharing in the positive energy of their accomplishments? Do we wish others misfortune or fortune? Do we seek to criticise or to compliment ourselves and others? All negative thought contributes to the deepening of the fractionate state. All positive thought centered on unity leads to the empowerment of joy and love in your life, moving you towards a wholeness of being. Making a positive conscious contribution to *all* life allows you to receive it back tenfold. So, if we have the awareness that we are all One, all possessing the same properties at the core of our being, then we cannot become disconnected unless we choose to. And yet, the fractionate state is the most common state in which people live. We may be fractionate because we are told or consider ourselves to be greater than our neighbors, and we may become fractionate if we consider (or are told) that we are not as good in whatever shape or form as the next person.

The fractionate state is a conscious agreement with inequality.

Contemplating fractionation is something which can provide us with a clear appraisal of our individual state of being at a time when we are approaching a mass awareness of possibilities in which humanity may consciously evolve.

CONSCIOUSLY EVOLVE?

We are entering a period long awaited by many cultures throughout the past millennia. It is an age when the opportunity to leap forward will be revealed to the entire race. This process of evolution is actually speeding up because it is no longer purely a system of natural genetic selection, but one of conscious evolutionary change, because we are presently choosing the future reality of our state of being.

Unlike all other forms of life, human beings are blessed with the ability to discern the truth of existence, to understand the individual parts of us that taken together make us a whole, consciously evolving each part to its highest potential.

We are not just bodies. We are minds as well, and should we open ourselves to the choice, we may become something that is greater than both body and mind; we may become One with the Source or Universal Consciousness.

Of course nothing is new, and we only now begin to feel the urge to leap because of the long run leading up to the coming jump. And it is coming. It will not be the last leap, but it will still be a gigantic surge forward in consciousness because it is a leap of conscious choice.

We live in an age when we can access the awareness of the higher possibilities of human consciousness in sufficient numbers to allow an escalation or outpouring. The spiritual consciousness is spreading like wildfire across the world because these are the last days of our old beliefs, the new days of spirit meeting the progress of science. They herald the possibility of what may be described as the next stage in the consciousness of humanity.

We all know that we can improve the world which we inhabit. We can improve our thoughts our words and our deeds, and in doing so evolve a part of the whole. So seek peace, seek to share all we have with others in order to put an end to suffering and inequality in the world.

For coming from the one Source, we are One.

When we judge, we judge ourselves.

When we congratulate, we congratulate ourselves.

We are a living sea that cannot be separated.

We flow to and from the Source of All Being.

Lost in time yet present in eternity.

It is not the source of the water that wonders if the sea exists, but the stream that seeks to know itself, for the Source is all-knowing, all-loving.

When we feel weak and unable to be what we know we can be and what we know that we are, take strength in other examples of our being, for this is how we have evolved, by a conscious natural selection of what was truly significant and sustainable. We are all streams of consciousness flowing with freewill, with many varied journeys, yet One destination.

Every emotion or mindset we choose to follow is reflective of our state of awareness. In daily life we need to understand that emotions and thoughts escalate positive or negative conscious growth because they are real, they are energy. When we say we 'can't help it', we are only deluding ourselves. We really can help it. Whether we are in a cycle of hate, fear and revenge, seeking to judge or blame, or experiencing the joy of life, love and being, we can be aware of ourselves, conscious of where those emotions and thoughts are emanating from, and seek to change them if we don't like them.

There is no reason why you need not like yourself, because you can choose who and what your-self actually is. It's your choice. If you want to change your old ways, your patterning, then you should seek to consciously evolve.

Forgive yourself and all others. Choose to change. Being honest with yourself and attempting to analyse your thoughts, emotions and actions, enables you to realize change for the better, allowing the budding flower of the positive spiritual being that you are to bloom into beauty in the world.

For at some point in our evolutionary cycle we will all realize a state of One-ness. Some have done it already. You can too. Many more are about to accomplish it; and eventually this transformation will be realized by *all*, for the benefit of *all* and in the process consciously evolve the world that we all inhabit.

The transformation to One-ness is possible because the miracle of you is possible. The joy of life lies at your feet. The wonders of nature are there to inspire you. Developing your consciousness will not only take you away from the dependence on your body but will replace what previously existed with a fullness of higher being, which will transform yourself and others and will consciously create a better world for our children and our children's children.

You are that fullness, for you are that higher being.

We can speculate how we might appear at some point in the future, how we might think and how we might look, but the fact is that we will evolve to the point where we return to the Source that we all came from. The origin of *all* life and creation. We will do all that is necessary in order to provide the greatest possibilities for our evolution, paving the way for the future possibility of unification.

To consciously evolve is a natural process. Every minute of everyday we send messages to ourselves in the form of conscious energy. We are either creating positive (evolutionary) thoughts, negative (devolutionary) thoughts, or are contemplating, or perhaps idling in a neutral or automatic state. These thoughts help regulate the rate at which the atoms of our being vibrate and the subsequent energy we radiate.

We must ask ourselves if it is true that we are the beings endowed with choice, then why would we choose to disassociate ourselves from the greatest positive potential of our species? The only logical response is that there is an obstruction. We are obstructed by the 'self,' an obstruction created by a personal choice of the mind. The 'self' hinders conscious evolution because it is self-ish. It cannot distinguish between needing and wanting. It wants to have for the sake of having. Oblivious to the possibility of becoming awakened to true being, it is your dysfunctional consciousness. To counteract this 'self', we need to focus our minds on our needs and the needs of those around us, allowing positive growth towards the wholeness of being.

One simple way to detract from 'self' is to try as often as you can to imagine yourself in another's shoes. When talking to your partner, your children, your workmates, your friends, visualize that you are talking to yourself. Be respectful of their words, thoughts and deeds. Treat them as you would want to be treated, as an equal. You will soon find that their reaction to you is changing. Your 'self' still seeking difference and separation, will not like this and will go on vacation... for a while at least.

So, in summary, we may aspire to seek those thoughts that are positive, that are of our 'higher' nature, and in doing so inspire ourselves, which in turn will inspire others.

When we truly seek the best in ourselves, we become truly conscious of our potential.

Being centered on 'self' and floating in our 'lower' nature, we resemble isolated drops of rain whose spiritual potential is eagerly evaporated by the heat of the sun. Aware of the One-ness that interconnects all existence, we become part of an infinite sea of transformation and change, the rolling tide of evolution.

WHY NOW?

Evolutionary change is an ongoing phenomenon, but it is rising to the height of awareness in our consciousness for good reason.

Resoundingly, the year 2012 has significance for millions of people. The Mayan or Mesoamerican Long Count calendar predicts the equivalent date (in our Gregorian calendar) of the 21st of December 2012 as being the end of a cycle of time. Interestingly, it is also a time of major astrological conjunctions, a shifting in the magnetic poles of the Sun and our subsequent exposure to greater amount of solar energy. 2012 will also see a very rare (once every 26,625 years) perfect alignment between the Sun, Earth and the centre of the Milky Way.

The writings and prophecies of diverse civilizations such as the Ancient Egyptians the North American Cherokee and Hopi Indians, the Dogon of Africa and the Inca of South America, all reveal 2012 as something fundamentally important to ALL mankind. Sacred prophecies abound for this universal timeline with descriptions such as 'Preparing to awake' or "The Age of finding ourselves again".

What is already occurring is a merging of the physical and spiritual realities through changes in our consciousness. More people are becoming 'spiritual' in their outlook, often making life changing decisions on the basis of feeling, rather than objective thought. Humanity is seeking to evolve.

2012 is the end of a cycle of time not the end of time itself. For when one era ends, another begins and we are arriving at a gate in time that provides us with an opportunity for change. It is our choice. Evolution or extinction, it is that simple.

Whatever happens in the future will be a direct result of the state of consciousness of the inhabitants of our planet.

Learning to develop reason beyond objective thought will allow the creation of a positive future for ALL of Earth's inhabitants.

Do not be slowed with concern yourself, for this is a reflection of fear, but apply a specific pattern of thought to the date 2012 that helps everyone, which is love. In this way we can allow positive conscious change to occur.

Throughout the ages, our schools of thought have been dominated by the concepts of punishment, control and redemption. It was thought that through the application of fear, we would react in a way that was morally correct and sustainable. Of course, when full of fear, we react like an animal would; only thinking of 'self' and of saving 'self.' When we are full of love, we realize the interconnectedness of all creation and the full beauty of life, that everything moves within a symbiotic relationship of One-ness; that we are all One.

What we have discovered as the truth is that we cannot fear something that we do not give our attention to. So if fear invades your mind, withdraw the attention from the focus of that fear and it will disperse. If we can focus on fear, we can focus on the opposing pole of unconditional love and we must learn to focus on love for all.

Likewise, withdraw the attention from the trapped mind of the 'self' and you will find the place where the truth of ALL being resides.

The year 2012 is about a shift. How we experience that shift and our consequent reaction to it, will be guided by our own understanding and awareness. Some see 2012 as meaningless, others as Armageddon. We might prefer to explain it as a window of potential, a portal into a new consciousness, a gateway into a new world arrived at by awakening to the reality of our true selves. Whatever we understand it to be, the timeline of 2012 will mark a convergence of consciousness. A meeting of our past, present and future. A blending of prophecy, spiritual awareness and rare astrological events.

The tide of change is inevitable and we are all a part of that process.

What is clear is that the world is rapidly changing; and as the consciousness of humanity struggles, so the Earth struggles to keep her balance.

If you want to make a difference, begin with yourself; create your own peace and harmony by freeing your consciousness from the control of the 'self'. Then share this new found freedom, for this will create a vortex of energy from where positivism can travel throughout your being, your family, the world, the Universe, throughout all existence. Inspire change by example. This is spiritual pyramid selling which everybody needs, everybody can afford and everybody benefits from.

We have always existed and will always exist, for we are not just bodies, not just minds, our primordial state is that of consciousness or spirit.

To fully comprehend where we came from is in itself a difficult task, because we, and everything that ever was, are all derived from the same One-ness. We can focus on our animal attributes, our analytical attributes or our spiritual attributes, but they all share the same universal source. Only One source of life exists, the Source of All Being, and we are continually evolving towards understanding it. When we choose to seek the spiritual content of our being, we begin to realize a connection and understanding of our true nature, grasping the significance of our greatest potential.

The awareness of our whole consciousness will help us control the mind and the body, so we should trust it, allow it to become our wavelength, permitting us to flow naturally. By doing so, we will undergo transformation on an unimaginable scale. We will see that we become tuned to the natural flow of the Universe, allowing our own consciousness and that of others to utilize and share exactly what is needed to evolve. In order for this to occur in our daily lives, we need to clear the way for self transformation. We need to stop worrying about the meaningless things in life. To try not to dwell on our problems, for they too will pass. To decide and distinguish the difference between our actual needs and our apparent wants. To be clear and transparent with our intentions, for intention is everything.

Learning to become aware of the existence of the conscious mind beyond 'self' and then gradually bringing that vibration to a greater resonance is paramount in learning to trust in that part of us which is undeniably good, our true nobility, our spirit. One way of bringing this to awareness is through meditation. Written below in italics is a short example of this. * Please note you may well find this exercise easier with a friend reading and guiding you through this visualization.

Imagine that the real you, your true being is able to release itself from the confines of your body. Visualize the crown of your head opening up. When you are ready, allow yourself to energetically move the vibration of light and energy that you are, your true radiance, out through the top of your head. You are leaving your body. It is safe to do so.

Up and up you go flying like a bird. Higher and higher still. See the clouds, feel the warmth of the sun. Rise above the clouds; look down at their incredible variety of shapes and sizes. Carry on still further until space beckons you. You look back and see the beautiful planet Earth. You carry on, farther still, into the great cosmos beyond. Then you gradually slow down, finally coming to rest. You are there. You are where you need to be. You are in deep space surrounded by utter peace and harmony. There are no interruptions, no distractions. Just peace. You are neither a planet nor a star; you do not need to be anything. You are space itself. Feel the beauty of the space around you. Here, you are at one with all consciousness. From here you begin to understand the meaning of eternity and the reality of consciousness beyond form. Feel what you are. Breathe what you are. For this is the real you. The eternal you.

Hold this feeling for as long as you are comfortable with it. When you are ready, reverse the process and come back down from space, to planet Earth and back into your body.

This exercise provides you with an insight to the higher states of consciousness, awakening you to the vibrations of the eternal being that you are.

The mind needs to experience a new vibration before it will accept it. Our focus then becomes a form of quality control and by continually trusting not just in what we see, but in what we feel, we open a door of awareness to the timeless state of spatial consciousness.

Chapter Two:
SPATIAL CONSCIOUSNESS

We can define human consciousness as being made up of three interlinked layers which can be described as;

- **The instinctive or body consciousness.**
- **The objective or mind consciousness.**
- **The Universal or spiritual consciousness.**

Transcending our objective mind consciousness we can arrive at a blending of our physical and spiritual states. This is what we call **spatial consciousness**. In our most efficient state the higher vibration of consciousness leads the lower, so that the physical mind can control the body and yet the spiritual mind or consciousness can control the body, while at the same time leading the mind beyond its preconceived limits and restrictions.

Utilizing this state of consciousness requires perseverance but everyone can awaken to it. **And that is exactly what it is, an awakening of your consciousness to the spiritual truths of your being.** Becoming conscious of the real you. No longer dependant just upon accumulated repetitive thought but on inspirational feeling. Losing the negative aspects of your being and replacing them with positive dynamic qualities that inspire both yourself and others. When we experience the reality of this state, we grasp the potential in ourselves and the evolutionary possibilities for ALL mankind.

Recognition of this consciousness occurs when we awaken to the prospect of the existence of an elevated consciousness that exists not just within, but beyond the body. The existence of awareness beyond our instincts, beyond the objective 'self'.

For all space is interlinked by One consciousness.

We, like all matter, are almost entirely made up of this same space. Therefore we are very close to being identical to the furthest star or the deepest parts of the cosmos, or the very air we breathe. Contained within our being are the identical elements that can be found within ALL existence, for everything is inextricably linked because we are all One.

By awakening to this eventuality we touch upon attributes that permit a marriage between the being we are and the higher vibrations of space. A blending of the finite bodies we are with the infinite qualities of the Universe. The reality that we can develop an awareness of spatial consciousness is another area where the advancement of science meets the totality of consciousness.

This awareness allows us to be conscious of our own degrees of consciousness, awakening us to that space beyond ordinary objective thought where we can become aligned with our highest potential. It is this dimension that we can employ to enable us to discern truth, reality and the states of being. Without the development of this ability, we will not be able to truly understand that which has happened, is happening or is about to happen. In a spiritual sense, we can compare this to the difference between the knowledge of the mind and the wisdom of consciousness.

Knowledge is the ability to record in our memory details that we have learnt to reproduce, through repetition, very often to prove or create. A store of detail if you wish, from which we struggle and work hard to find something new, more perspiration than inspiration. On the other hand to develop wisdom is the ability to instantly expand upon knowledge via the tool of consciousness, manifesting in order to establish new awareness, thus evolving previous thought in our most efficient manner.

We may equate the potential of spatial consciousness to the existence of alien cultures in the Universe. If we were a highly advanced evolved race of alien beings (and of course at some level of our awareness of being One we might well be), would we think that we had to create metal spaceships to travel the length and breadth of the Universe, seeking to explore or destroy other forms of existence? Or would we have evolved to a level whereby we could understand the laws of the Universe and the connections existing between all? Would we be so evolved compared to humans that we would realize that our connection to each other was through the consciousness, the spirit, a union that could not be divided by anything, and use this universal system to send out messages of hope, love and possibility to the entire cosmos, feeding the present wave of evolution?

We are not alone, just as you are not alone.

One thing is for sure, we may have different bodies and minds, but we are all of one spiritual substance or universal consciousness. If we had reached the zenith of our development and advancement, we would be consciousness or spirit itself. We would be neither visible nor invisible. We would know that our evolutionary destiny was to become one with ALL existence, that spatial consciousness was the key to union and survival. If we could move throughout the Universe via the stream of consciousness, we would not need to 'move' an inch, but would contribute towards the greatest momentum.

Here on the beautiful planet Earth, we are realizing an approaching time when we will be able to understand more of our reason for existence. This point has been reached now because the process of evolution has already developed the human body and substantially improved the potential capacity of the brain. Our least developed asset is our spiritual consciousness, the ability to recognize and utilize our connection to spirit. There is a certain urgency to move now because of the escalation of the present cycle of extremes. The irrationality of war, terrorism and global warming are examples that are closely linked with the chaotic states of impaired awareness in the world today. On the other hand, it is the arrival of this same chaos that encourages the current wide scale spiritual awakening. For the world we live in is changing at such high speed that it has pushed spatial consciousness to the fore. We are evolving in order to survive.

Should we step beyond the weighted mass of our forefathers, into this new perception of living life in communion with all existence, then we will begin to touch upon the spiritual truths of creation.

THE WEIGHTED MASS?

This refers to the physical body and genetic material that all humans have. At this time, it is a necessary evolutionary requirement to have a body! We must learn to share the awareness of the gifts that the body provides and come to terms with the burden that the mind and body can create when allowed to do so.

The many centuries of ignorance of the perception of 'purity' has only led to more confusion and frustration. Clearly, we cannot ignore the functions or needs of one part of our being in order to elaborate others, for this will eventually lead to chaos. We must take good care of the body and the mind, for they are the vessels of being and consciousness. It is only through a healthy balance between the body and mind that we will absorb and retain the higher states of our being. From the long range perspective of our ongoing evolution, we clearly needed to have a body to be able to understand what it was, how to evolve it and one day how to evolve from it.

As with any focus of attention, if it becomes a habit in our everyday thought, then it becomes very difficult to abandon. The same applies to the process of leaving the shell of the body, 'passing out' of this world.

'PASSING OUT' OF THIS WORLD?

Yes, when we pass out of 'this' world, or die, the consciousness of our being undergoes a transformation. Physical death, as we understand it, is the loss of consciousness of our nature as a body; and yet coinciding with this 'loss' is an expansion in awareness of the finer forms of consciousness, partly because we realize that we continue to exist without a physical body.

If, at this point, we are aware that we are not only that body, then we can continue to evolve without the need for that body. However, if we see this point as the loss of all our material possessions and of our perceived life, then we enter a transitional period of necessary reawakening.

There are also many who are so attached to the world of physical matter that they find it exceedingly difficult to transform from one state to another, to leave behind the material world, because they have not learned to withdraw attention from the 'self'. What they own, their roles in the material world, the house they live in are what they consider to be their true selves. Even after leaving their body they remain focused on the 'self,' still wanting to have more, still putting themselves first.

There are many who are traumatized by the reality of their own passing, existing in a state of turbulence; but we can all be transformed when we choose and learn to focus on the ocean and not the drop, on the idea that our lives are necessary experiences from which we may develop a deeper awareness of ourselves.

We can experience another side of this focus through our awareness of the concept of reincarnation.

For some it is difficult to contemplate having led a previous existence for it denies the pre-eminence of the present 'self'. For others, a need to accept the laws of reincarnation is strongly linked to the longing for the desired continuation of that same 'self'.

It is what we say and do in the now that reveals true being to the world, not apparent previous position or future status.

Keeping with the principal spiritual law of 'We are All One,' there will eventually come a time when there will be no need for the continuation of the individual presence, for the universal consciousness is a unified state, evolving as One, not consistent with the attachment to separation and form existing in a lower state of vibration.

For we are many bodies, yet One spirit, One truth, One light, existing on the many planes of being.

As the present blossoming of spiritual awakening continues, the developing human consciousness pushes to outgrow the old order and arrive at a new stage of wisdom and awareness. The alternative is to continue to perceive that all existence belongs in some form of hierarchy. This is a trick of the mind of 'self' and the world of matter, utilized by the dysfunctional consciousness of those seeking a negative fractionate state. It is from this position that some become 'empowered' in the world of matter, seeking to control others in order to satisfy their self-ish needs. They accumulate material wants while at the same time dissipating spiritual needs. In the spiritual reality no hierarchy exists, for the evolution of the individual paves the way for the evolution of the whole.

Spatial consciousness exists in eternity beyond the claws of matter, out of reach of the destructive hands of time. Spiritually, all of our abilities are identical and only our present awareness is different.

So, as we spiritually grow, we may arrive at new stages of understanding the true nature of our being. This does not mean that we were or are the only being to arrive at such a point of awareness. We are just one of many individual yet interconnected souls who have reached what 'appears' to be uncharted territory, but in fact shares that discovery with others that pass, have passed, or will one day pass that way.

The journey to becoming more conscious will take us through many states or dimensions. Essentially, we may begin to develop our higher mind via the ladder of consciousness, to the point of absorption where our new vibration takes over from the old patterns of thought and instinct. Becoming no longer dependent on, attached to, or confined by the world of matter, we are moving to the new reality of spatial consciousness.

At an indeterminate point in our growth, we may be able to allow this consciousness to function through us as we continue to lead a normal physical existence in the world. The more we are able to live with this, the more truth and manifestation that will thrive in our lives and in the lives of those around us. Truth will become more apparent in our outlook, our words and thoughts; and less importance will be placed upon the world of matter, mind and emotion. So that in fact, we will reach a state of balance and detachment, which will allow us to react in a natural, controlled way to any occurrence.

We learn that the irony of the world we inhabit is that matter does not matter, that emotion does not always have a notion of true reality.

When we arrive at this awareness of One, we reach a point of understanding where we no longer have a need to consider ourselves as being separate to anything. That all things truly are One. We realize that energy is eternal and since we are partly energy ourselves then we are partly eternal. But which part? The unified state of spatial consciousness transcends time and is not susceptible to wear and tear. It is a part of our eternal being, a doorway to eternity. By recognising and developing this consciousness now, we are in effect consciously developing our souls; for it is the resonance of our state of being that dictates our position or locality in the Universe. We may also realize that we are here in this present form to evolve our individual state of being, which in turn expands the light of awareness, thereby helping us to help others, for that is the very nature of the spiritual beings that we truly are.

Our physical form allows us understand the laws of nature; the mind allows us, if we so choose, to understand the nature of ourselves and others, and consciousness allows us to awaken to our true presence. We become bearers and sharers of light, present in our most significant state being aware that what is within is also without. We have, at this point in our growth stripped away the clouds of the 'self' to allow the sunlight of our true being to manifest.

By having no need to be important or different, we touch upon spiritual insights that are potentially transformational. Withdrawing from the wanting nature of the 'self' allows us to receive what we really do need, which is to become more aware. We discover that we can utilize a greater consciousness for the benefit of ourselves and *all* others.

For it is only by giving that we may truly receive, and only by receiving that we are able to give.

This is the 'reality' of the spiritual rebirth that we undergo when we seek the evolution of our awareness. The stages see the recognition of levels of being, greater and lesser, higher and lower, as we begin to purify ourselves.

When we evolve to a height where love and light may be drawn through the windows of the soul (the eyes), then we will no longer have a need to justify 'self,' for we will no longer be separate, but whole. Look in a mirror, deep into the centres or pupils of your own eyes. Looking deeper still you can see that the eyes are a visual representation of creation. They hold the truth of your being. They are the meeting of the void and matter. They hold and display a recorded imprint of the 'Big Bang'. When we 'fill' ourselves with spatial consciousness, the eyes become one of the natural outlets for this awareness to be dispersed into the physical world of matter. When we become immersed in this state of being, even the awareness of our individuality may appear withdrawn, for we are at One with all being; conscious of our connection to Source.

By accepting the Oneness of the love of all being, we transcend old patterns to allow collaboration with the vibration of creation, the Universal Consciousness.

We no longer have the need to think or to be, but are.

We are not what was, or will be, but are.

As with all spiritual lessons and experiences, there will be times in our development when we will waver when approaching a new awareness and it will take time to harness any new energy. By seeking more and remaining aware of our weaknesses, we will be able to master ourselves, in turn sharing a greater awareness of the whole, escalating the present level of awareness in the world.

It is our responsibility to seek our true birthright that has been hidden from us by a part of our very own nature, for the lower vibrations of our being have denied us the truth. As we begin to rediscover the potential of our existence, the lower resonance is worn away and reshaped transforming old into new, body into mind into spirit.

We may or may not feel that we somehow lived a previous existence, that we have a connection to somebody famous from a past life, or that we were humble, unimportant souls. These feelings are somewhere in the deepest memories of our minds. It does not make sense to us when we look at our body, so we mostly ignore it. Whether we think of ourselves as this person or that person reincarnated, is irrelevant when we see that we are all One, for being One gives us access to all memory, all lives to be felt, tasted and enjoyed.

If we have access to the significant reality of anything that ever happened, then the need to assume form is redundant. Form is associated to the world of matter and we gain far greater awareness of the reality of our existence when we deny the importance of 'self,' one of the most persistent manifestations of form. In the higher truths of spiritual consciousness, 'self' does not exist, for the focus on 'self' has been withdrawn, and the 'selves' merge to become One.

We must make the fundamental truism of we are all One rebound in the hearts and minds of each other and then we will truly realize our transformation.

Motivating ourselves towards transformation allows us to achieve true sustainable spiritual change of the highest quality.

For this is how we expand our individual drop of consciousness, allowing ourselves to flow downstream to the sea, evolving as part of the whole. For true transformation to occur, it requires a blending of mind, body and spirit. This experience must be resoundingly felt on and impact all levels of our being. For repeatedly reading, listening to, or reciting something does not make it transformational.

We must foster the intention of the proposed action, in order to receive the proposed gain. When we follow the process through and benefit from the gain, we will find that it vibrates throughout our being. This is what transformation does; it brings us closer to feeling the truth in the wholeness of our being.

Chapter Three:
TRUTH IN OUR TIME

When we devour a statement with our intellectual mind, we may seek to agree or to disagree with it. We do not always look for truth; often we seek something so that we can prove how competent we are, or how less capable others are, how our 'self' has a superior value to another's 'self'. At some point however, we become aware that any element that creates a split or diversion in our world is in fact a destructive force, an expression of negative energy that is contrary to spiritual needs and only contributory to the fractionate state.

The list of these divisive elements is extensive and familiar, and we have no need to refer to it, other than to say if we let our focus dwell on unity, then we will find it.

The immense gains in wisdom, equality and reason by the Ancient Greek civilization serves as one example of the evolution of truth in our history. By allowing more time for their minds and more space for their consciousness to explore the nature of all 'things' they built a school of philosophy and a new state for all. A new state of awareness. From this awareness came a greater understanding of mankind and the cosmos.

The truth of spiritual awareness is revealed by awakening to a higher plane of reality where there is no more 'self,' allowing only one conclusion; that 'we' are all that exists in the unified mind of 'God'.

Each child is a miracle and each miracle is in the child. Seek your truth in the innocence with which you were born, for we are all connected.

What is the apparent truth (that which we are led to believe by the 'self' as being true) will not necessarily be the apparent truth tomorrow, but what is the actual truth (real truth unaffected by the distortion of the 'self') was and always will be part of the whole truth, for it is not subject to change or misrepresentation by time, only to differing levels of perception.

She flows throughout eternity untouched and pure, an occasional advisor to the finite, eternally faithful in her ingenious word.

When we feel the truth, it comes closer, like the invisible force of a powerful magnet, all the time pulling us to its source.

Have confidence in your awareness of truth, and rest assured that it is not yours and yours alone, otherwise it would not be approaching truth.

APPROACHING TRUTH?

Spiritual truth can only be approached by the mind when we choose to operate our reasoning from beyond the control of the 'self', by transcending objective consciousness. The high vibration of spatial consciousness provides us with a truer perspective of overall reality because the arrival of reason is no longer inhibited, manufactured or tarnished by the dysfunctional 'self.' The mind learns to adapt, forming a new perspective of the reality of things, becoming conscious of the whole and sympathetic to all parts.

Absolute truth comes from the infinite heart of creation. Being the finite matter that we are, when we seek and find a truth, we can only explain it in the terms available to us, and in doing so we lose the purity of the experience, because we bring it down into the form of matter. In becoming matter, it becomes finite and so loses some of its purity. Truth can be shared on all levels of our being to transform ourselves and others. We can only be party to this truth if our intention is to share and not to teach.

Spiritual 'teaching' requires a distinct hierarchy of levels or degrees of capability, whereas in fact all spiritual capability is identical and only the present awareness is different.

The present state of the world serves as a reminder that we are still allowing ourselves to live in conditions that are well below our potential.

THE PRESENT STATE OF THE WORLD?

The upheavals in the world today reveal that there is a definite battle going on, a battle of hearts and minds, greed and control, poverty and excess, and perceptions of right and wrong. At its core, though, it is a battle we are fighting with ourselves.

We cannot be in a state of harmony unless all play a part in recognizing the actions of the whole. This is certainly not reality in the world today. The existing state of the world is something that we have brought upon ourselves. Now don't worry, we're not saying that we are guilty. We have the chance to learn and to evolve, transforming our world, as others in far off galaxies are doing and have done with theirs.

We have brought this state upon ourselves because we have raped and pillaged the body of the planet that we inhabit. We have confused and distorted the minds of the inhabitants. But the connection to spirit remains unchanged, for it is truth. What we are doing is allow-

ing ourselves to become detached from the higher beings that we are. The body and mind are realizing an opportunity to steal what is not rightfully theirs, to debase our true selves.

In the physical world we do not seek to harm ourselves, and if we do, we may be considered insane and removed from society for treatment.

So why do we continually seek to harm ourselves then? Constantly seeking membership in the most powerful group, striving to have more than our neighbor, feeling that color depicts ability or position, that sexual orientation is good or bad, or that a father spiritually knows more than his son, when we are all cut from the same cloth and there are no Masters or Neophytes, just brothers and sisters.

Realize this and we may peek across the mountains of possibility, down into the valley that awaits, the truly promised land, the place where all are brought together by following the 'Path' to where we can live in the most natural way suited to the core of our being.

Chapter Four:
THE PATH

We must travel towards wherever we need to be, in doing so we are on the Path. We are searching for what we need to find, but we must not forget that the light of spirit is within us, as is everything we will eventually need to have or understand. By turning inward, we will begin the greatest journey outward that we could possibly imagine.

By seeking others we will find only others. By seeking ourselves, we will discover *all* others.

We must not ignore the truth that we feel, for that is our Path, and when we wander down we must wander wholeheartedly. Sometimes, in our humble understanding, we will lose our way, for that is our Path. And when we wander, we may have deliberately taken a mistaken route in order to show ourselves the right way.

There is no good or bad journey, but when we are blind, we stumble aimlessly, desperate to find our way. We remember all significant experiences so that we can share them with each other. Nevertheless, we must return to cure our blindness, so that we can continue getting to know ourselves.

The Path is all about finding our own route through the complexities of life. How successful we are travelling that Path will depend on what dimension of consciousness we allow ourselves to be guided by. Clearly we are all on a journey called life, but if we cannot understand or awaken to our destination, then the whole process must either be about 'self' enjoyment or be completely pointless. Sitting here, watching the vines sway in the gentle breeze, two tall trees standing proudly in the middle of the vineyard, the sun shining down enriching our lives, we cannot contemplate that all this was pointless or centered on the 'self.'

The point of creation was to share.

WHAT ARE SIGNIFICANT EXPERIENCES?

Significant experiences are those which are transformational.

At the end of our physical lives, we can only look back at the true significance of our existence by reflecting upon not what we have done for ourselves, but rather that which we have done for others.

What we have done for others, we have truly done for ourselves, for we are parts of a greater being, we are all One, and we need to see and feel the significance of that in our daily lives in order to proceed.

Our awareness is to share all significant experiences.

When we go through a truly significant experience, we should not keep the treasure hidden, but muster the will to share it.

For the treasure we seek is the wisdom of knowing oneself, in order that the house of self may be put in order.

Far better to be rich in spirit than to be possessed by

your own wealth, for that is the nature of the material world; it is a world of possessor and possessed.

When we possess material things, we become possessed by them. So we should seek those things which are true and ineffable, that are unchanged by the passing of time.

When we realize that we are all One, we realize that we will never be alone. We have all we need, and so does everyone else. We don't need more than our neighbor, but are propelled to share so that we *all* have enough and in doing so live up to the loud voice of equality that is inherent in our spirit. The three realms of being (body-mind-spirit) provide many different ways in which you may share with others, so that *everyone* has the ability give or share in one way or another.

But we must learn to use the tool of consciousness in order to adapt ourselves better, to become the higher beings that is our spiritual birthright.

Consciousness is a field of vibration that exists for us to explore in order to evolve, a tool from which we can begin to comprehend the true nature of ourselves and of all things.

It is through this amazing spiritual dimension that we may create.

We may have no awareness of this, and we might feel that we are singularly responsible for our gifts or talents. Or we may see the work of an artist and claim them to be the greatest that ever existed; but in all cases we were and are responsible for every invention and creation, because all manifestation comes about by passing through consciousness to be received by the mind, in order that it may be shared with the whole.

It follows the route of consciousness to mind to body.

This does not mean that we should attempt to take legal action against Thomas Edison or Alexander Graham Bell. But it does mean we are connected to them, and were connected to them when their inventions were conceived. Neither does it mean we should not say thank you to these and other pioneers. But it provides us with an awareness of how all things came about, and how things will come about in the future. When we see that the end result was brought about via the universal consciousness, then we may understand the way in which this cycle functions.

SO ARE WE CONSCIOUSNESS?

If we consider that we are drops of water in the ocean, we cannot claim to be that ocean, yet we can claim to have the same properties.So it is with consciousness, we absorb more or venture higher depending upon our receptive ability. The greater our connection, the more 'conscious' we become. We must understand that the use of consciousness is a way in which humanity can unite, for when we explore deeper into the nature of consciousness, we can only come to the same conclusion that we have come to since time began, that in some distant point in the past when we came into being, we all came out from the same void. It is the body and the erratic, egoist elements of the mind that seek separation, that search for a fractionate state that is converse to the loving, nurturing, purified state that, as we gain further awareness to the potential of consciousness, is revealed as the great unifying possibility.

Chapter Five:
OURSELVES AND OTHERS

One day we will all unite; it is inevitable, as all things return to their source.

Why are we then choosing the road of separation? Is it because we do not want to share with others what is ours? Because we think that we know better? Our intellect is far superior? We have nothing to gain from sharing? We are better looking? We are taller? We are thinner? We are sexier? We have struggled for what we have? Our family has worked hard for all this? We really need to earn more money? Our skills are unique? Our gifts are unusual? We are special?

We must understand that we are no worse or better than anybody else, for we are all reflections of each other. We are all One.

When we talk of others, do we seek to mention the greatest assets of their characters, or the faults that we appear to see? Do we wish them every success and mean it? Are we honest with them and ourselves?

If the situation was reversed, it would make for some very interesting observations. So that when we talked about ourselves, we would immediately list all the faults of our character. We would want ourselves to fail, or even seek to confuse ourselves. This is the present reality of the judgmental world where we live, where we seek to justify our presence not by seeking the reality of that which is in all, but by dwelling on that which makes us feel better about our 'self'. In this state we seek fractionation and not unification.

WHY DO WE JUDGE OTHERS?

We may be judging others to enable us to say to our 'self' that we are better or in someway superior to those we are judging. We all do it; we all have done it. It provides us with comfort in the safe bubble of 'self' where we reside. When we absorb more consciousness we continue to do it, until we arrive at a stage of awareness that may balance our entire being.

When we arrive at the awareness of One, then we see there is no need to judge, that superiority is a concept of the ego, that being judgmental proves that we are trying to give 'self' value by pulling others down, which as a matter of spiritual irony, may mean that we also stop or slow down our own spiritual progression.

If we have any real worth, then we are able to perceive and acknowledge worth in others. When we can see the worth in others, then we are truly worthy ourselves. When we can acknowledge the light in another, then we are truly enlightened.

So let us look at others in the way we would like others to look at us, for the beings that we are, and not what we appear to be. Not what the apparent whispered rumours say, but for our thoughts, our words and our deeds. We know what we are, for we are true to others in order to be true to ourselves.

"Now that we are beginning to know ourselves, we are beginning to understand you."

SO IF WE ARE ALL ONE, WHY ARE WE SO DIFFERENT?

Physically, yes we are different, mentally, yes also, but on the spiritual level, we are all the same, for we are all One. Spiritual Science reveals to us not just to look 'at' the body or 'above' the body, but to look 'under' and 'into' the body. Looking at the construction of the human, contemplating the atomic and sub-atomic structure, drawing from the similarities we discover existing between all universal matter. We then find that quantum physics provides us with information that we already know, if we only trust our true selves.

We are atomic. We have the ability to change our atoms. When we change our atoms we transform from one state of awareness to another, and consequently through the increased immersion in spatial consciousness, we are able to bridge the gaps that may be found in the synaptic spaces of the brain, connecting existing paths into the awareness that we are all One.

We cannot see it or measure it, yet we trust in the existence of it, for we discern the truth of its existence.

When we can see our true selves, that is an achievement.

When we can see ourselves in others, that is awareness.

When we can see that everything lies within everything else, then we are free of the restrictions of the singular, fractionated mind that we no longer need.

We hold *the awareness of One.*

We choose to operate our mind in a different fashion that allows the free flowing energy of spatial consciousness to connect that which we previously thought to be impossible. Everything is possible when we touch the eternal consciousness of all love, all knowledge. Nevertheless, humility of character is a disposition that we must continue to hold.

So seek to be whole, for that is why we created our-

selves, to experience the journey, to test our resolve, to marvel at our inventions, to be lost in the visual beauty of an emotive work of art, to soar with the pulsating rhythm of the music, to sense and touch the splendid magnificence of mother natures' creation, but most of all, to discover our true selves, to be made whole once more, to find you, to find me, to light upon an understanding of the eternal truth; We are all One.

THE AWARENESS OF ONE?

The awareness of One is a thought process that allows continued existence in the consciousness of 'We are all One.' It is a tool of thought that we can apply to the mental state to not allow us to falter on the wave of spatial consciousness. When we begin to approach the growth or expansion of our consciousness, we move forward, but sometimes we arrive at areas or times of inaction.

These are called plateaus, and exist for good reason, to enable us to absorb the new level of consciousness, to absorb into it, to resonate with it, until it blends with our state of being becoming our new vibration.

When ready to move again, we allow ourselves more consciousness, arriving at another plateau, to rest and contemplate before beginning the cycle of movement, absorption and resonance once again. There comes a point when we sense the need to stop the emotional and mental upheaval this causes to the mind and to rest in a state of consciousness that allows a platform for stable, continuous growth from where we can operate. This is what we call the awareness of One.

We must hold the possibility of this consciousness and develop it as part of our everyday thought structure.

It must become our mindset, so that we can transform ourselves.

If we can draw a circle in our minds eye, we can visualize the energy of One.

If we can visualize the energy of One, we can sense the energy of One.

If we can sense the energy of One, then the energy of One is reality.

When the energy of One is reality, this is shared with every living thing. There is no choice, for the nature of this awareness is inclusive and complete.

It cannot exclude itself, for in itself is everything.

It either exists or chooses not to exist.

We are all One and we choose to exist.

We choose to change the world in the most beautiful way and for the benefit of all, for becoming conscious of the One-ness of existence and retaining that awareness can only lead to an outpouring of positive transformation in the world.

In remembering the awareness of One, we simply return our minds to the symbol of the circle. The circle that contains all. All of life, past, present and future exists within this perfectly round figure. Recalling your place within this One-ness allows a corresponding match between yourself and the vibration of infinity. Being whole and complete, there is no need to contemplate anything beyond the circumference of the circle.

Once we arrive at the platform of this awareness of

One, we have no more need for choice, because our choices were already made a long, long time ago. So we must follow what we set out for ourselves in order to transform, to create a new world. We have observed enough of the human 'animals' with minds that have created wave upon wave of death and destruction in our world.

The universal and spiritual laws do not permit destruction, but transformation from state to state. We transform ourselves in order to survive. This is the real truth of natural selection; as a race of beings, we are consciously and sub-consciously selecting which transformation we see as the process that enables continuing evolution of our species, and these changes are carried out via the principle of the weight of perception.

Chapter Six:
PERCEPTION AND EXPERIENCE

When a thought or concept 'arises', it does so from consciousness, appearing as what may be considered to be the thought or dream of an individual. That thought then energetically 'grows' and becomes the hopes and aspirations of a few, then of many, until eventually it becomes accepted by a sufficient number of minds, becoming accepted as reality.

This is the way in which manifestation occurs in the universe.

So, if we adhere to the methodology of We Are All One, then we can only introduce those things that are beneficial to all of us and not just good for one or some.

The weight of perception allows us to understand why,

if we were not aware or chose to ignore the awareness of One, we might consider ourselves as individuals to be the creative genius of the dream. This might be our explanation to ourselves and others, as we fell into the evident ego trap of the complacent 'self.'

We have ignorance and clarity as we have the fractionate state and the awareness of One-ness.

Whichever we align with, we utilize.

Whichever we choose, we become.

Whichever we agree with, we understand.

That which is seen to move the least creates the most response.

The resonating atom forms energetic groups with other atoms, according to their vibration, connecting and affecting, becoming manifested quantum change. They are energy becoming matter, having the properties of both waves and particles. We cannot see what is behind the construction of the atom without applying change or transformation. But when we do, we find that the atom is made up of the three parts it needs to be, in order to become a whole atom, a functional building block of universal matter. The atom consists of electrons, which carry a negative (-) charge, protons, which carry a positive (+) charge and neutrons, which carry no charge or are neutral (0). All parts have different qualities in order to produce a balanced whole.

Likewise, there are elements within our being, and within all that exists, which pose the nature of increase, the nature of decrease, and of a neutral nature, all combining to exist as in the form of the unification that we call matter.

How does the atom group itself into matter? We can understand this by the application of the principle of the weight of perception, the more aware we become, the more efficient our atomic transformation. In terms of conscious evolution, we may seek to experience and develop knowledge of all of our parts, for only then can we approach the fullest potential of our being. By looking carefully we start to realize that the circuit or 'poles' of +, 0 and − are not only within us, but existing at the heart of all things.

One interesting area of atomic research in the field of

quantum mechanics is the 'measurement problem', for science is still at odds to explain how it is possible that atoms themselves react when being studied by man. So the tiny atom, measuring just one millionth of a millimetre across somehow reacts to being observed. Is this suggestive of an elementary form of consciousness? Do all atoms have the ability to 'read' and react to exterior sources of energy? Nor can quantum physics explain the mystery of the nature of the particles or fields that generate what is called vacuum energy. The clearest understandable example of this is the Casimir effect, whereby two metal plates are held or suspended facing one another. After some time, they are seen to be naturally drawn or to bend towards each other, because of the resonance of the energy fields in the space between them. Science is beginning to teach us that ALL matter, visible or invisible, appears to 'own' or 'attract' fields of energy. At some point in the study of the atomic and sub-atomic levels objective consciousness goes out the window to some extent. Developing the science of quantum physics alongside the potential of consciousness can only lead mankind into a bright new age of discovery entering the area of Spiritual Science whereby we may 'discover' that above all measurable energies and fields there exists a One-ness, where ALL existence may be seen to be unified.

The neutral theory of evolution, as theorised by Motoo Kimura in 1968, explains that the great majority of evolutionary changes are not caused by Darwin's law of natural selection, but by the random drift of selectively neutral mutants. Awareness shows us that this 'drift' is selected by the weight of perception, the accumulated movement of consciousness. We may see from this example that we are choosing what we become.

By choosing 'self' we remain fractionate, dysfunctional and ill; but via the awareness of One, we are becoming whole, consciously evolving.

SO DO WE CHOOSE TO BE ILL?

Yes. We can choose to be ill. We may have chosen to become ill before the illness manifested itself in our bodies. If we began the process, then we can provide the solution to the problem. For if we can make ourselves ill, we can make ourselves well.

You see the spelling of **I**LL? The letters it contains? The spelling of **WE**LL and the letters it contains? When we sense the awareness of One, we do not choose illness, but we may become aware that suffering serves as a catalyst for arriving at a greater awareness by causing us to study ourselves, by helping us to improve upon what we discover.

It is the 'self' that allows illness, the mind causing the body to react. However, the benefit of illness in the process of evolution is undeniable, for we can only evolve by experiencing the negative and positive, exposing ourselves to the choices in order to seek the preferred route of existence, to learn what works and what fails. We already have an awareness of all of this, yet we need to recall it.

There are even those amongst us who seek illness or disability in order to enable them to share the awareness of One with us all, and these are among the most humble.

For everyone and everything has its place, for this is the whole.

There also exists a school of thought that says that reincarnation and inherited illness are interlinked. But we may see that the awareness of reincarnation exists to provide us with examples of how we are all reflections of one another, that the appearance and action of a handicapped or disabled person is most often misunderstood by those who are fractionate themselves.

Do not be misled by apparent differences, for they only serve to distract you from the reality of spirit.

EVERYTHING HAS ITS PLACE?

Each aspect of our being seeks to raise consciousness, for this is the key to evolution.

There are those of us who are unaware of this. There are those of us who are aware of this, who seek to hold on to the powerful feeling. There are those of us who are aware of this and seek to share it in order to evolve the whole.

Consciousness in metaphysics is one example. Channels, healers, psychics and mediums use the evolutionary tools of consciousness.

Nothing has all the answers, except when it is the whole. We can only seek the whole when we are unified.

Each process of awareness requires tools and skills to evolve towards our potential, which is that of becoming One.

For instance, if we are what we call psychic, we can raise the consciousness of another person by providing information about them that is helpful and positive, which can be interpreted as incredible and amazing.

If we are what we term a spiritual medium, then we can evoke the consciousness or spirit of a person that has passed on, to enable a message of hope and positivism or a message of love to be delivered to the surviving relatives, which in turn relieves their suffering and raises their consciousness.

If we are healers, we can allow enough spatial consciousness to flow directly or indirectly through the recipient in order to infuse wellness, provided that they are open to receiving this.

If we are channels, then we can absorb information from consciousness that could be beneficial to those already aware that they are searching.

These are the ways of the mystic beings that we all are.

If we hold the awareness of One, then we are harnessing the spatial consciousness in our body in order to bring about transformation. It is not something that we use only when needed, for it has become our consciousness. This awareness provides examples of inspiration that can give rise to transformation in others.

None of our roles are better or worse, greater or lesser; for they are the roles that we need to see and experience, in order to evolve ourselves further.

Of course, the more aware we become, the more awareness we can find.

We can watch a film, read a book, sing a song, share a joke, look at the incredible array of stars in the night sky;

we can look at each other, or simply contemplate a stone. It is only our mind that tells us it is complicated. Our spirit knows that it is the most natural simple element at the heart of our being.

By sharing the awareness of One, our consciousness will undoubtedly be raised. We will begin to seek pleasure in the simplest things. In these cases, we are helping ourselves to help us all.

If we cannot see why we are doing something, then that is where our awareness of it is. If we know why we are doing something, then we know that we can achieve the intended result. We also know that we can stumble and fall along the Path; yet if we get up and try again, we will return to the possibility of what we set out to achieve.

We continue throughout time to lead our existence and learn the lessons of the past, evolving, transforming mind and matter into reality, learning how to evolve, remembering our past experiences to keep ourselves aware of the underlying truths of our existence. And here we are today on the threshold of such a rare experience that we cannot but help to feel the butterflies in our stomach.

How much better are today's computers than the first computers? They have evolved. We have evolved them. The same applies to cars, houses, airplanes, telephones; yet we are seeking that which we cannot find in the world of matter because it is not a material reality, but a spiritual reality.

We are inspired, enthused by consciousness, the vibrating wave of potential.

When we all have what we all need, then we will want for nothing, but what do we all need? That depends on the alignment of our consciousness.

What does an explorer truly seek? What does an artist seek to paint?

If our alignment of consciousness centers on 'self', then we require material substance that provides the appearance of having succeeded to our 'self' and others, giving the impression of having accumulated more than them. We may allow our minds to tell us we need this accumulation, or that we deserve it and that is true for us at that stage, but it is not in itself an answer.

One tool of the awareness is to imagine that everything you own is no longer yours, then to ask yourself what is left.

If you own nothing, then nothing owns you; and you may begin to realize what you actually have that is of significant lasting value.

If we hold the awareness of One, then we seek to unite under one consciousness, one world, one universe, one truth.

We may feel that this is beyond our grasp at this time, but we know it is not. Every second of everyday we are evolving. Some of us may be still, some of us may be busy, but we are all undergoing conscious change at some level.

The weight of perception in the world is building; approaching a time when the movement of the interconnected cogs in the clock of awareness cause the bell of conscious evolution to chime, marking the hour of transformation.

We are not alone, we never were. We will have all the

help and assistance that we require to take this leap of faith, for would we not give ourselves as many chances as possible to shift and adapt in order to survive?

WE ARE NOT ALONE?

Consciousness is a medium that can connect all parts to a whole, a One-ness.

To think we are the most superior form is ignorance. And this ignorance proves to us that we have not yet found our own form of clarity, the expression of our higher selves.

We are surrounded by many forms, some of which we may not see, but only hear or feel. This is because each area or part of our mind-body-spirit being has the capability to receive the awareness of different frequencies as a way to constitute reality. Even our left ear receives information at a different frequency than our right ear and it is the resulting blend of the two that provides us with what we perceive as sound.

Even the sound you hear is but a part truth, a blend

of separate realities providing a uniform impression of wholeness.

When the awareness of One is firmly held in our consciousness, then we become aware that what we perceive as living reality is that to which we are attuned through our understanding. If we can comprehend the existence of any form of matter, then we can accept its reality. If we allow ourselves to comprehend the life that we cannot see, our awareness will shift so that we can experience it.

We might be able to see or sense the etheric energy around the body, part of what we now commonly call an aura, to see the microscopic beings that fill our air, we might be able to see or sense so much or so little, but we will perceive what we need to receive to enable our evolution to continue. What slows our evolutionary path is when we ignore or repeat what we have already learned, or when we revamp what was already true, for then we move into a state of frustration and confusion.

We start thinking that we are new. We are not new, for we are as old as the hills, and we are in the process of realizing this fully. Whenever something of a pure or high vibration manifests itself in the world, we tend to copy or take part of that concept or experience for ourselves as individuals in order to create a new version. The more it is copied, the less like the original it becomes and the greater the snowball of confusion.

Looking back at the history of the spiritual evolution of the human being, we may see that there were individuals who were able to inspire great transformation, challenging the past beliefs of society. The repercussions of these transformations are powerfully present in the world today, even after the passing of hundreds or thousands of years.

We may see that the law of conscious evolution acts no differently than the law of natural selection, in that the teachings of any individual who reaped benefit for the whole -- Krishna, Buddha or Jesus -- became consciously sustained through the weight of perception; for this imparted wisdom contained a sacred reality available to all people, a greater awareness of existence beyond 'self', the existence of the presence of something greater than man.

Looking back at them, we may develop the awareness that these individuals were all a part of an eternal conscious evolution.

The evolution of consciousness provides examples in order to provoke growth towards the Oneness, the Source; just as physical evolution provides the manifestation of a genetic freak in order to evolve a species forwards.

When humanity becomes confused by the world of matter and mind, then consciousness steps in to guide us with whatever means necessary, to open our perspective to the new. What was heretical may therefore become conscious reality.

Humanity has time. Consciousness has eternity.

Spiritually, there is nothing new, but we are sometimes unable to see that. If we are unable to discern reality, then we are confused about the nature of the truth. All the latest spiritual fads, names, theories and beliefs are old or new variations of previous philosophies. All the discoveries we think we make, we had already discovered, for they emerged from the outpouring of the universal consciousness before they became physical reality.

As individuals, seeking truth may be a very difficult process and so we must learn to discern the realities to all areas of our being.

HOW DO WE LEARN TO DISCERN?

We learn to discern by feeling truth, such as, what the nature of matter is and what the formless state of spiritual truth is. We cannot discern spiritual truth by sound, smell, vision, taste or thought, but we can by spatial sensing, by learning to trust in our higher senses. When we do this, we become focused about the spatial concept of truth and apply no preconceived picture to that thought; but we are still, seeking the clarity that only consciousness may provide, the peace of the stilled body and mind.

There are those who seek to feel the existence of their own belief. There exist those who seek to disprove the beliefs of others. Both instances are fractionate states. But we may also seek to unify belief, by discerning the truth in all.

From this void of untouched space, we can learn to feel and discern what truth there is in what we see, hear, think, and read. But we must learn, by combining all the layers of our multi-faceted being, to sense to what degree truth exists in our experiences.

Spirit is truth, which remains unchanged.

We know all about ourselves, our highs and our lows, our greatnesses and our weaknesses, for it is all part of the same sea of Oneness that has existed throughout the ages.

It is through the shifting of the tides of perception that the next truth begins to surface. Sporadically washed up on the shore of reality, moved betwixt the sands of time, the flotsam and jetsam of consciousness gather, witness to the existence of all that is contained within the single ocean of the One-ness called life.

The pressure is building. We are experiencing more and more diverse reactions on all levels of existence in the world today. We can choose to look the other way, denying the existence of the problem, or we can cut straight to the core. When you live in and so condone the fractionate state, be that individually, as a select group, or as a collection of favoured countries, you are excluding others. Why are you excluding others?

If something is right, it must be right for us all or it will be wrong for some and therefore indicative of the fractionate state.

Truth, and our discernment of it, is an evolutionary process for the whole.

Examples of higher consciousness have come and gone and will continue to do so, because they carry that message or underlying truth at the heart of all existence, that We are all One, that 'you' and 'me' are a spiritual 'we'.

It takes time, but the awareness of consciousness gives us the opportunity to have access to the entirety of our being, the Source that we came from, the All that we are and the return to Oneness that is to come. Trusting in our true selves we know that we will receive all we need to in order to succeed.

For all we really need to guide us is truth, and that is what spirit is, the truth in us.

BUT WHAT OF THOSE WHO AREN'T INTERESTED IN TRUTH?

We do not worry that some of us do not realize or seek a truth at this time, for that is a necessary process in order to reveal that very state to ourselves. Those who are not interested in truth are not interested in life outside of themselves at this point in their evolution.

If we seek to develop a sense of truth, then we become aware that we are part of the weight of perception, a possibility of change.

When we constantly seek to ignore the truths confronted by our senses, at some point, the law of cause and effect will show us the way to proceed.

When we constantly seek truth, we begin to recognize more what it feels like, because our focus is on it.

We become our focus.

WHAT IS OUR 'FOCUS'?

Our focus is our ideal, or that aspiration we carry in our hearts and heads.

The focus gives rise to the energy that provides the answer.

That is why focus is so important to us, as it defines our reason for being who we are at this time.

When we understand that we are all One, then our focus is to hold the awareness of One, so that we can transform ourselves, fulfilling our evolutionary purpose. We no longer hold the desire to define or be defined.

We become aware that position and praise are as fleeting as matter, that perception of spirit and truth is paramount in how we begin to transform ourselves. Spirit and truth cannot be corrupted, or sold, or altered. They are the infinite spatial qualities that we can all share.

Chapter Seven:
SPATIAL QUALITIES AND THEIR USE

Spatial qualities are those attributes that develop from spatial consciousness, those qualities or fields of energy that exist beyond the state of matter, resonating at a higher frequency because of their potency, for example: TRUTH, LOVE, WISDOM (Understanding), ETERNITY (Infinity).

All of these qualities have the same essence of timelessness and truth, for they are pure and unchangeable in their highest form. As human beings we contain trace elements of these spatial qualities. In order to consciously develop, we focus on them in order to absorb more of them. They are not wholly part of our being because of their higher frequency, but they can be brought into our being in order to transform it by consciously seeking to rise to their vibration or resonance.

When we recognize the existence of these higher frequencies, we begin the entrainment of our frequency of being, which is an absolutely natural process. The phenomenon of sympathetic resonance shows us how a motionless violin string comes to life when the equivalent note is played on a piano. Likewise, we align the vibration of our being to that resonance we recognise as belonging to our true selves.

We seek to join or to 'tune into' this higher resonance, for these are the qualities where we came from and to which we will return to one day. That is why they allow us to feel positively good when we experience them, even in part.

We might see that the process of evolution for humanity is based on the concept of rediscovering the root of our being, transforming ourselves in order to live outside of matter, eventually becoming pure spatial qualities ourselves, and in doing so, returning home, adding our part to the whole via the weight of perception, thus beginning to realize the fullness of being.

Through repeated use of verbal affirmation, we can open the consciousness to its ultimate possibility. Bearing this in mind, we may choose to repeat the following statement:

"WE ARE THE SPIRIT OF LIGHT THAT RADIATES LOVE AND WISDOM THROUGHOUT TIME AND OUR HOME IS TRUTH."

We gain most awareness about raising our consciousness when we believe what we are saying. Through repeated use of phrases or mantras we can become aligned with the words by the concentrated focus of attention. Beyond this, discerning the words to be true allows their power to manifest in the aspects of our being.

The use of both prayer and meditation is a fundamental way of raising our awareness of consciousness. They have similar properties. When in a deep state of prayer or meditation, we have our eyes closed in order to dissolve the world of form that we sense is not our only plane of existence. This enables us to create an awareness of reaching that state or vibration which we understand to be of a higher nature, the nature of true reality.

CAN WE USE THE FOCUS OF ATTENTION TO HAVE MORE?

Yes, that is its purpose, and the meaning of that will be understood by your own state of awareness at this time.

It is not the purpose of this book to focus on the accumulation of material things, but to seek the fusion of spiritual ideals. We seek to stir consciousness into an outpouring of positive transformation, nothing less. When we contemplate this, it is not intended for any single individual, but for all of us, because we are all One.

There are numerous books that have evolved us through these stages and we can see that many were based on receiving for our own benefit in the physical, mental and emotional planes. But ask yourself this, when you appear to look perfect, when you have all material things, all the intelligence you want, what will you truly have? We say that you will have what you wanted and what you sought.

If you find happiness and peace of mind, then great, share it, for these surely belong to all. **Nobody can really 'give' you anything, but you can give yourself all.** When we focus on renewing our consciousness, we will learn to find our true selves.

This book concerns spiritual gains, for if you are focused solely on physical gains, spiritual rewards will elude you. If you are centered on conscious spiritual evolution then you will receive more gains than you can possibly imagine. You will have more than you could ever have dreamed of having. Learning to transform our consciousness can be enhanced by studying the examples we find in the world around us.

Let us look at transformational processes occurring in nature, for again we can arrive at the place where science meets spirit, creating a spiritual science, if you wish.

When we consider osmosis, we can compare the action of this process to the way in which we accumulate our awareness of consciousness:

"Osmosis is the movement of a solvent across a partly

permeable membrane, from a region of high solvent potential to an area of low potential, resulting in a concentration gradient."

If we dwell on the awareness that we as bodies are semi-permeable, like a type of membrane, and the 'solvent' is consciousness, then this moves through us from the most aware area or point of reception, to the least aware area of our consciousness, until we reach a point when we have absorbed enough, where we are full, until we are ready to grow again, for consciousness, like the process of osmosis, is about growth.

We cannot see osmosis with the naked eye, but we can understand the process and the end result. We cannot see consciousness but we can understand the process and feel the result.

There is a natural process of balance within the process of osmosis, as there is with the absorption of consciousness. With both it is the quality of what we are absorbing that creates the defining balance within the body. If we look deeper still at the process of osmosis and its effect upon cells, we may see that fundamental to the process are three reactions that occur.

These are: the hypotonic, the isotonic and the hypertonic.

Hypotonic reactions result in a gain (+) from the process, isotonic reactions result in no movement (0), and hypertonic reactions result in a loss (-).

We can again see that the building blocks of cells, like atoms, seek the same balance of positive, negative and neutral in order to create a whole. As the cells and atoms of our being retain the properties that we absorb, so we have the capability of retaining the feeling or resonance of the source of consciousness, allowing it to become a part of our state of being.

This is the most evolved purpose of focusing the attention, to change our atomic and cellular structure via the absorption of a higher vibration of consciousness, to consciously evolve.

We may arrive at this awareness in many ways, and this type of positive interchange may be provided by anything, but the higher the vibration, the greater the energy of attraction. What causes our consciousness to rise contains the greatest potential for transformation.

POSITIVE INTERCHANGE?

The positive interchange of consciousness may be understood as the receiving or sharing of awareness, wherein we naturally rise to meet that with which we have a sympathetic resonance, or receive a reflection of that to which we are already attuned.

The more consciously aware we are, the less matter we require to study or contemplate, but the more we comprehend.

We have already touched upon the One-ness of the circle and the power that it may have to alter our state of consciousness. The power of the triangle is another positive interchange, for this may be seen to depict the flow of energy to provide power to the whole.

This can occur in the individual, with body, mind and spirit.

Or in an electric plug, earth, live and neutral.

Or manifestation in the universe, from Source to the point of delivery to the whole.

Once the process has started, it is aware of its function, intention and goal, and so only requires time to become reality.

We can feel the uplifting movement of energy when we enter a place of beauty and calm, or in the message we intuit when we look deeply into a work of art, or even from the beautiful simplicity of a child's drawing. The creative arts, competitive sport, faith, the bird in the tree, the bee collecting pollen, these all provide potential for exchanges of consciousness. We will find it wherever we need to find it. Human beings do not always share the same experience of how and when we recognise it, nevertheless, we all may find it if we allow ourselves the possibility.

The many varied forms of the positive interchange of higher consciousness include the simplest of experiences such as laughter or the joy expressed in the recognition of a connection between friends. It is something we can all experience when we share an association that brings us 'out' of ourselves, freeing us from the insular protective shell of the 'self.'

That which lifts us up from our 'self' is the connection to a higher plain of consciousness.

This exchange is what inspires us to evolve for it provides us with great expectations for the future. It is the connection we feel when we love one another, the heart or center of all of our hopes and dreams. This is the process of positive interchange, the way of approaching our potential, the experience of spatial attributes at our current level of understanding.

Positive interchange allows for the positive flow of consciousness to move toward us, providing awareness that there is something far greater than 'self,' something whole and complete, which we seek to realize. When we look beyond the spatial qualities for their source, we can see that the source of all truth, all love, all wisdom, eternal life, is the formless void, the 'God' of our understanding.

Chapter Eight:
GOD OF OUR UNDERSTANDING

The 'God' of our understanding refers to our own comprehension of the divine sacred. The existence of an all encompassing unified reality continuing beyond the world of matter, surpassing both the limits of time and the confines of space.

It does in no way apply to a single religion, but to all religions, all beliefs.

"It is not important what we call God, but that we call" George Harrison said.

Keeping an open mind to the truth in all religions allows us to perceive that each era and system provides insights into an underlying, evolving reality. Defining a particular realization of 'God' in the world of matter directly limits the understanding that we may potentially develop.

On reading the name 'God,' we may immediately create a mental image of a separate being or of a divinity of a certain gender. But instead let us contemplate the spatial qualities of the 'God' of our understanding. Before the arrival of shape and form, before all time and space began, there was 'being' and from this 'being' sprang forth all planes of perceived reality.

So in remembering 'God' we recognize the universal reality, the ever living, ever loving reality that was, is and always will remain the 'Source of All Being.' This is the 'God' of our understanding. With no needs or wants and no requirement of retribution 'God' is a naturally evolving universal presence at the heart of everything in existence. We will understand all this in alignment with our spiritual awareness. The more we focus our attention on seeking to discover the nature of 'God' the more it will be realized in our lives.

When we align our consciousness to the spatial qualities of the 'God' of our understanding, we begin to deepen our awareness.

By allowing the 'God' of our understanding to become the focus of our attention, an impression of the divine will be revealed to us. Through the Awareness of One, we may realize that everything is interconnected and be able to hold a higher state of consciousness in order to contemplate the matter further. In this way, we may see the truth of what we seek to understand.

SO WE MAY SEE GOD?

We may see 'God' or not according to our needs and our awareness but we can all be aware of him for we are all a part of the same One-ness. This 'seeing' is related to how conscious we are, how much spatial consciousness we absorb and how much of this becomes the focus of our attention. Some of us at this point may seek for the proof of the awareness of 'God' and others may reply: **Consider the**

love you have for your children, you know it is true and absolute; and though it is not visible or tangible, it cannot be denied, for it is truth. We are in the time of truth, a time when humanity must look itself in the mirror and reply honestly.

HIM, WHY NOT HER?

This is metaphorically speaking for it is not a question of gender, although *everything* contains a balance of gender. Only by blending the male and female energies together can we grasp the whole reality of gender, providing ourselves with the unified neutrality of truth as shown in the simple sum $(+) + (-) = (0)$.

We return to the spiritual science that reveals to us that any whole is made up of these three parts. If we equate this with our awareness of the gender of the 'God' of our understanding, then we can see that the All Being of 'God' must be composed of a collection of both feminine (-) and masculine (+) energies in equal, unlimited amounts, thereby creating a neutral (0) balance. For the accumulation of true spiritual qualities is not limited by gender and yet the whole cannot be reached without the participating role of each part.

So 'God' is all gender, for it is all.

What is interesting is what gender the many different descriptions of 'God' provide to our consciousness and that throughout history we found it necessary to define divinity as being gender related. This again indicates the evolutionary stages that faith and religion have passed through, for we can see that for there to be one source and us to be emanations of that same source, we must all have the properties of that source, so that source must contain *all* the combined possibilities of gender. So we may be a blending of male and female energies in terms of bodies, minds and spirits, each having subtle energy differences which combine to reveal the individual being.

We may also trace the evolutionary process of consciousness through the power of religious symbolism. Each era or school of thought seems to have a symbol that provided a conscious understanding of the divine. By understanding the meaning of those symbols we approached the underlying reality of the Source of All Being. We became more conscious of the reality of 'God.'

The existence of crop circles, however made, is a present day example of consciousness being expressed and shared. The real power and true meaning of these symbols lies far beyond their artistic value for they are vibratory emanations assisting us in becoming more conscious of 'God.'

CONSCIOUS OF GOD?

At some point in our awareness becoming conscious of 'God' or 'God conscious' is what the process of an evolving spiritual life is about, evolving to involve ourselves with the mind of 'God.'

Everything is conscious, the sky, the tree, the bird, the worm.

They are less conscious than the human being. They have little or no choice; but nevertheless they are conscious of 'God' to a degree for they are part of that Source.

To be conscious has a wide variety of meanings. In one sense it can equate to just being, in another sense it can mean having an awareness of our surroundings. It can also mean having the awareness to study oneself.

This is the blessed opportunity that humanity has, to study itself and aspire to evolve. We know that we do not have to be aware of something for its properties to be within us. Although of course those properties are there and remain there until they are rediscovered, when we are awakened to their existence.

So when we seek to become more conscious we do so in order to evolve our being to the state of becoming One within the mind of 'God.'

ONE WITHIN THE MIND OF GOD?

By being at One within the mind of 'God' we may see that manifestation is transformation. We may arrive at the understanding that we are sharing the consciousness of 'God,' that "love thy neighbor as thyself" was a great necessity and indeed the only possibility. That getting to know or sharing our true selves was the purpose of creation.

When we talk of being, this is what real being is, being in the mind of 'God' where growth and consciousness are One.

The awareness of One is a powerful transformational tool that helps us to realize that all men really were created equal because in the truest sense anything else would be an absolute impossibility.

The world of form is vibrations that we grow through in order to allow our own expression; "Seek and you shall find." By seeking our 'self' we find our true selves.

To be at One has no greater meaning than to be One with all existence.

To be aware that we are all One is refreshing to our spirit and something that we have earned. We have all earned all these things. We have earned the opportunity, the possibility and the right to be true to ourselves when we say "We are all One."

We have seen our failures, our successes. Evolution can

only occur in relation to experiencing these poles of failure and success.

Being at One within the mind of God allows us to see that the Universe is living mind, an expanding thought in the process of evolution.

When we are ready, we will pull back, withdraw, and one chapter will be closed. And another one will begin, for that is the nature of infinity. This is the time when we stop and think. That requires us to withdraw from the mind of God or to reassess our state of being.

Likewise, involution will be that time when the mind of God stops and thinks about how it arrived where it is and takes another breath.

We need to share with ourselves to evolve to our highest potential, to find peace in doing so and trigger the connection in the universal mind that we are satisfied, that our evolution is in the process of fulfilment.

On that day, everything will be without shape or form. Matter as we understand it will cease to exist. Harmony will be a sound that reverberates throughout a timeless, formless void and we will truly understand.

For the process of sharing experiences is what we require in order to remember the whole story. Evolution is all about memory. We cannot forget those who have given so much. We are One with them, they are with us; they came from us and came back to us.

Don't seek to understand what you cannot understand. Seek your 'self'; for in finding your true self, you will find the answer to any question, the key to any mystery, the reason for being. So seek the mind of God, for that is where all reside.

IF WE CAN 'SEE' GOD, THEN WHAT DOES HE LOOK LIKE?

The mind of God encapsulates everything, the manifested and the un-manifested all rolled into One. The dream and the reality, all One. The body and the spirit, all One.

When you go to sleep at night and turn off the lights, look up into the darkness, look deep into that darkness and look past that darkness and when you are ready you will see the light. If you meditate, close your eyes and do the same. Look into yourself, then deeper still, past the depth and there you will find the light that indicates the way.

When we are ready, we receive all that we need.

If 'God' really is your focus you will find him, for you will see him everywhere and you will reveal to yourself that love alone is not 'God,' but instead that love is a spatial quality of his being.

The same applies to all of the spatial qualities. They are part of the whole, and the power lies not in the individual part, but in the whole. Growth, after all, is not confined to one seed, but to the whole universe. So 'God' encapsulates all spatial qualities, for that is what the Great Spirit is.

If we can understand one quality and consciously manifest it, then we are manifesting a part of the whole, we are spiritually advancing.

Becoming aware of and manifesting one spatial quality provides example for others to manifest more spatial attributes. That is the way of spiritual evolution, paving the way for others in order to evolve the whole.

The greatest examples of spiritual manifestation in history have provided a physical outlet of spatial qualities. Humanity has frequently been unable to recognize their truth at the time. More often than not they have realized more of that truth at a later date.

These qualities have remained inherent in our thought because they contain the perennial wisdom of not one man or woman, but of the Universal Mind. They are unchangeable through the passing of time or through the part-truth of one school of thought, for they are truth, they are spirit. Having evolved through the cycle of consciousness, humanity cannot distort them, for they are untouchable, they are of 'God.'

Chapter Nine:
LOVELIGHT AND HEALING

As we have seen, when we are most aware of consciousness, we are most aware of our true selves. The process of the cycle of consciousness is a wave of energy of which we become aware. We have seen this in the process of absorbing into consciousness, resonating, resting and the theory of the plateau.

This is the cycle. We may perceive the reception of this in the form of a wave of energy. The wave formation is the way in which the infinite reaches the finite. We can envision this process as spirit to mind to body. We move with that wave formation, following its cycle, the cycle of consciousness.

In order to manifest transformation throughout our being, we seek not just to 'ride' the wave, but to 'hold' the wave. We still seek the absorption into the awareness of consciousness; but now we seek the neutrality of holding the resonance.

We do this by being aware of the wave, by riding it, then absorbing it; but also by not coming all the way back down with it. We seek to consciously hold our position in the wave, for by doing so we transform the way in which we accumulate more consciousness. When we perceive the arrival of a new wave, we must look to absorb the highest peak of it without allowing a return to the same waveform with which we were previously aligned. We seek instead to find a more efficient way of growth. Once we can do this, the wave becomes less and less acute until at some point, we arrive at complete stillness, a state of no mindful activity, with no needs or desires, just free and unified with the One-ness of all existence, the final resting place in the conscious evolution of the human being.

This process may take millions of years or one second, for the more we do for each other, the more we find of our true selves.

Human beings are more than just animals with great minds; we have between us all developed a greater awareness of becoming conscious. We have revealed more consciousness to ourselves. This is not a process that can be reversed, for it is an ongoing expansion of awareness.

Involution occurs when the weight of perception, the awareness of consciousness has filled so much of humanity that a return journey is then possible. We may liken this to a magnet's forces being reversed, the new resulting charge being an opposing polarity to the previous field of energy. But between evolution and involution, we reach the outer cloud of the nucleus that denotes the ending of one evolutionary phase and the arrival of a new dawn. This marks the pinnacle of our cycle of conscious evolution, a period when the lessons we have learned can become a reality in our world. At this time consciousness becomes most manifested in the physical world of matter, creating the reality of the greatest positive change for humanity.

This new dawn marks the arrival of a more evolved

human being, not disconnected from our previous existence, but evolved from us all, one that appreciates itself and all others.

It is a future time of joy, love and peace, when war will be seen as a monstrous relic that was a necessity of the past. Where peace of mind, body and spirit will be the most common thread, a golden age of unity long anticipated by humanity. Hate and greed will dissipate. People will no longer seek superiority, or to have more than one another. Everybody will receive everything they need, becoming enlightened within a 'new' consciousness.

All we require to manifest this future (what we are presently doing) is to bring it to awareness. When sufficient human awareness becomes aligned with this consciousness, the principle of the weight of perception allows it to become the new 'reality.' If enough of the parts recognize the truth in it, it will become a perceived truth; because not being conceived by the mind of the 'self,' it cannot be subject to the decay of the finite world of matter. Consciousness herself prepares indicators for us all, providing opportunities for the next step in the evolution of the spirit of humanity.

This type of manifestation of consciousness would not work if we said to ourselves we want you to carry on fighting, suffering, being ill, for this would clearly be originating from the negative fractionate state of the 'self'. In that case it would become a backward step into the devolution of chaos.

However, at this time, we are riding the wave of consciousness. We need to seek the foundation of steady, solid, efficient growth, or we will continue rising and falling from peace to war, health to illness and love to hate for longer than we need to, continually jeopardising the future balance of humanity.

Seeking our greatest truth provides us with the clearest answer.

LOVELIGHT: a poem of hope and peace.

Give us joy, give us peace,
Give us love and let all fighting cease,
For in this world,
There's not enough peace of mind,
What we need is a golden time.

With no more hate, no more greed,
No more fighting one another to succeed,
One and all,
Having everything they need,
It can happen if you truly believe.

Let the lovelight shine around the world,
And we will be living in heaven on Earth.
Let the lovelight shine around the world,
Just think what could be if it happened…

No more lose, no more gain,
Having everybody equal on one plane,

No more ill,

For we can do away with pain

When true love, peace and harmony reign.

Let the lovelight shine around the world,

And we will be living in heaven on Earth.

Let the lovelight shine around the world,

Just think what could be if it happens...

Lovelight refers to all forms of healing.

It is Love and Light, the dream and the reality of becoming One. Through this medium we may change the world. When we are aware of it, we must share it, we cannot hide the light. By truly utilizing this tool we adhere to the practice of becoming One and see the truth in the statement that we are all One. No longer confined and restricted by the 'self' that needs to be seen to be doing, we become true being.

We have not only found our outer and inner purpose, but also our nucleus, the reason behind the action, which is OUR purpose, for OUR purpose is One.

CAN WE KNOW MORE ABOUT HEALING?

Healing is something that we may practice according to our awareness and understanding. This may entail a thought, a prayer, working in hospital saving lives, or it may encapsulate empathy or love. It is our individual awareness of One-ness that allows us to express our connection to all.

Developing 'Lovelight' is a way of healing.

We do not need to spend a fortune in order to have some impressive certificates, because God doesn't do certificates. We might need to become sufficiently responsible and aware in order to heal, but we can all do it. True healing needs no name. We use names solely to create identification for explanation and clarification. By thinking of 'Lovelight' as a beam of many different rays we keep an open mind to the possibilities of how it may develop. It is a potentially high frequency or 'divine' healing method and is something that we may all utilize. The potency of any form of healing is most effective when it embodies spatial qualities. We are able to utilize Lovelight most efficiently when we can step aside from 'self' allowing the natural flow of the universe to radiate through us. We create the reality of stepping away from 'self' through a sequence of events.

1. *We promote the intention, that is to say we realize the existence of empathy between ourselves and the healee. We understand that we are seeking to consciously assist them improve their present state of being.*
2. *We relax ourselves deeply, ensuring that our 'self' is aware that it has no controlling role in the coming events. Our intention is to raise our state of consciousness to the space beyond the objective world of the 'self.'*
3. *We allow ourselves to reach that space of equality, love and light that exists beyond the mind of the 'self'. This is the spatial consciousness that exists beyond form itself. Conscious of the combination that pro-*

vides harmony to our being, we perceive the wholeness needed to be reinstated in each other.

The possibility of healing is open to all, manifested according to our awareness and understanding. It requires the discipline of looking within and without. The more we become aware of the ability, the less we require connection with the world of matter. If we were to dissolve the world of form, we would see that names are also applied to serve a spiritual purpose. If we seek to name a form of healing we must contemplate why we seek to name it, whether the answer to that returns us to 'self' or a combination of our 'self' and the whole, or that it takes us to the One-ness. This is what will define the potency of the healing. The greater the presence of 'self', the less effective the healing.

By sharing, we are learning to seek the higher essences of our nature and continuing to evolve towards the state of One-ness.

We are either not at the point of realizing that we may radiate a form of Lovelight or we are in the process of beginning to realize it; or we already aware of a certain form of it.

When we are aware, we have found something beautiful within ourselves that we seek to share, to help as we are helped. The greater our awareness of the nature of the healing, the more we seek to share. We know the body, the power of the mind, now we seek the spiritual truth behind the form.

At some point in our evolution we will manifest Lovelight of some kind. The greater awareness we absorb, the less we seek alignment to form and the greater alignment to spatial qualities occurs within our consciousness.

We cannot define the exact nature of Lovelight (that would provide limitations for the mind) other than to say that it will be the definition of healing with which we are happy, able to accept and which corresponds to our current vibration.

We can study this further when revealing to ourselves that Lovelight encompasses all techniques of healing. Let us suppose we contemplate a named form of healing which by nature, is a form of Lovelight, seeking to realize its evolved reality;

> Does this form have a name?
>
> Do you need a certificate to practice it?
>
> Can you teach it to others?
>
> Why would you teach it to others?
>
> Does that form of Lovelight have a copyright or trademark?
>
> Who owns that trademark?
>
> Is it a new system or method?
>
> What training does it require to qualify in the practice of it?
>
> How much does it cost?
>
> What happens to the money?
>
> Who developed it and why?
>
> What is different about this form of healing?
>
> What does it teach about self knowledge?
>
> What awareness does it provide that 'We are all One'?

Can you potentially live in that consciousness?

If not why not?

Do practitioners charge for it?

How much? Why?

Is that forming the latest thing?

Can it be made better?

Does it transform as well as heal?

Do we need it regularly?

How often?

Why?

Can it change our lives?

Can we practice it on ourselves?

If not, then why not?

Does it require the awareness of spatial ability?

What spatial qualities does it evoke?

Looking at the answers to these and other associated questions, we can reach an awareness of the state of the evolution in both the healer and the healing method.

Many of us seek to cash in our new found perceptions,

techniques or discoveries, but why is that?

Applying the awareness of One, we can see that we never really 'own' anything at all; we are just borrowing what belongs to the whole, while passing through.

Many of us seek to justify what we are with our qualifications, or by the impression created by the name form of our profession. In our lifetimes, many of us get stuck at one point of spiritual evolution because we become empowered in a false way; we have developed a high 'self' esteem, 'self' importance and 'self' value.

Who and what makes a person 'successful' is again a matter of awareness.

When we are 'successful,' and we look at what we do for a living, then what is the motivation behind our success? What are our goals? What is the driving force?

At this point, we would like to refer to an old Chinese proverb, funnily enough entitled "We Are All One."

Long ago there was a wealthy man who had a severe eye disease. For many years, the pain was so great that he found it very difficult to sleep at night. He visited every doctor in the area, but none of them were able to help him.

"What good is all my money?" he moaned to himself. He became so desperate that he sent messengers throughout the city offering a large reward to anyone who could help cure his affliction.

In the city lived an old peddler who sold homemade sweets. He would wander around the market with his baskets of sweets; but he was so kind that he gave away as much as he sold, so he was always poor. When the old peddler heard the announcement, he remembered something that his mother had once told him about a magical herb that was good for the eyes and decided to go in search of the magical herb so that he could claim the reward. He packed away his baskets and went back to the old, tiny house where he lived with his family.

When he told his wife about his plan, she scolded him, saying, "If you go wasting time on this crazy idea, what will we have to eat?" Usually, the peddler gave in to his wife in order to have a peaceful life, but this time he was stubborn. "We have two baskets of sweets left, and I'll be back before they're all gone," he said.

The next morning, as soon as the soldiers opened the gates, he was the first person to leave the city. He did not stop until he was deep inside the woods. As a boy, he had often walked in the forest. He liked to pretend that the cluster of trees was a huge, green sea, and that he was a tiny fish swimming through the waters.

Now, as he examined the ground, he noticed a line of ants busy working away. On their backs were larvae which looked like grains of rice. A rock had fallen into the stream, making the water spill all over the ant's nest.

"We are all one," the kind-hearted peddler said. He waded into the stream and removed the rock. Then with a sharp stick, he dug a little ditch so that the water would drain back into the stream, away from the ant's nest.

Forgetting about his good deed, he began to search the forest for the magic herb. He searched everywhere, but as time passed, he grew sleepy, and lay down in the shade of an old tulip tree, where he fell fast asleep.

In his dreams, the peddler stood in the middle of a great city. Tall buildings rose high overhead, and he could barely see the sky, even when he tilted his head back. An escort of soldiers marched up to him, their armor clattering loudly. "Our queen wishes to see you," the captain said.

The frightened peddler had no choice. He had to obey. The soldiers led him into a shining palace. There, a woman with a big high crown, sat upon a tall throne. Trembling, the peddler fell to his knees and touched his forehead against the floor.

But the queen ordered him to stand up. "Like the great emperor Yu of long ago, you tamed the great flood. We are all one now. You have only to ask, and my people will come to your aid."

The old peddler cleared his throat and told the queen that he was looking for a magical herb that would cure any eye disorder.

The queen explained that she had never heard of such a thing, but added: "You will find it if you keep searching for it."

Then the peddler awoke. Sitting up, he saw that in his wanderings, he had returned to the ant's nest. It was there he had fallen asleep. The city in his dream had been the ant's nest itself.

"This is a good omen," he thought, and he began searching with renewed vigor.

He was now determined to find the herb, and he didn't notice how quickly time passed. He was surprised to see how dark it was getting, and realized that he was now completely lost.

Night was coming fast, and with it the cold. He rubbed his arms and started to hunt for a shelter where he could rest the night. In the twilight, he thought he could see the tiles of a green roof. He stumbled through the growing darkness until he reached a ruined temple. Weeds grew through cracks in the stones and most of the roof itself had fallen in. Still, the ruins provided some protection.

As he entered, he saw a centipede with bright orange skin and red tufts of fur along its back. Yellow dots covered its sides, like dozens of tiny eyes. It was crawling into the temple as fast as it could, but there was a bird swooping down toward it.

The peddler waved his arms and shouted, scaring the bird away. Then he put down his palm in front of the insect. "We are all one," he said. The many feet tickled his skin as the centipede climbed onto his hand.

Inside the temple, he gathered dried leaves and found old sticks of wood; soon he had a fire going. The peddler even picked some fresh leaves from a bush near the temple doorway and placed them in front of the centipede, thinking that it may be hungry.

Stretching out beside the fire, the old peddler put his head on the pillow of his arms. He was so tired that he soon fell asleep, but even in his sleep he dreamed he was still searching in the woods. Suddenly, he thought he heard footsteps near his head. He awoke instantly and looked about, but could only see the brightly colored centipede.

"Was it you, friend?," the old peddler chuckled and, lying down, he closed his eyes again. "We are all one," a voice said faintly, as if from a far off distance. "If you go south, you will find a pine tree with two trunks. By its roots, you will find a magic bead. A cousin of mine spat on it years ago. Dissolve that bead in wine and tell the rich man to drink it if he wants to heal his eyes."

The peddler trembled when he heard the voice, because he realized that the centipede was magical. He wanted to run from the temple, but he was too scared to even get up. It was as if he was glued to the floor. But then the peddler reasoned with himself: If the centipede had wanted to hurt him, it could have a long time ago. Instead, it seemed to want to help him.

So the peddler stayed where he was, but he did not dare open his eyes. When the first sunlight glimmered down through the roof, he raised one eyelid cautiously. There was no sign of the centipede. He sat up and looked around, but the magical centipede was gone.

He followed the centipede's instructions when he left the temple. Travelling south, he kept a sharp eye out for the pine tree with two trunks. He walked until late in the afternoon, but all he saw were normal pine trees. Wearily, *he sat down and sighed.*

Even if he found the pine tree, he couldn't be sure that he would find the bead. Someone else might have discovered it a long time ago. But something made him look a little longer. Just when he was thinking about turning back, he finally saw the odd looking tree. Somehow, his tired legs managed to carry him over to the tree, and he got down on his knees. The ground was covered with pine needles and he was too tired to concentrate. The peddler could have wept with frustration, and then he remembered the ants. He began to call for them "Ants, ants, we are all one." Almost immediately, thousands of ants appeared out of nowhere. The peddler explained he was looking for a bead, and that it could be very tiny.

Then, careful not to crush any of his little helpers, the peddler sat down to wait. In no time at all, the ants reappeared with a tiny bead. With trembling fingers, he took the bead from them and examined it. It was orange and looked as if it had yellow eyes on the sides. There was nothing very special about the bead, but the peddler treated it like a fine jewel. Putting the bead into his pouch, the peddler thanked the ants and their queen.

Shortly afterwards, the ants disappeared among the pine needles, and he made his way out of the woods.

The next day, he reached the house of the rich man. But he looked so poor and ragged that the gatekeeper laughed at him. "How could a beggar like you help my master?" The peddler tried to argue: "Beggar or rich man, we are all one."

It so happened that the rich man was passing by the gates, and overheard the voices. He approached the peddler. "Alright, but if you are wasting my time, you will get a stick across your back," he said to the peddler.

The peddler took out his pouch. "Dissolve this bead in some wine and drink it down." Turning the pouch upside down, he shook the tiny bead into his palm and handed it to the rich man.

The rich man immediately called for a cup of wine. Dropping the bead into the wine, he waited for a moment, and then drank it down. Instantly the pain vanished. Shortly *after that, his eyes healed. The rich man was so happy and grateful that he doubled the reward. And the peddler and his family lived comfortably for the rest of their lives.*

This story has many meanings and as with all spiritual realities, we gain an understanding of its deepest meaning according to our awareness. Any form of healing, like the magic bead, has the potential of evolving to a point in our awareness where it becomes the spatial qualities of love and light that may be passed between people, a point of emission and a focus of reception. The power and effect of the healing may be immediate and sustainable. It may infuse both parties with the spatial qualities of love and light. We can learn to absorb and pass these qualities when we are free from the restraints of matter and of the self. When we are in this state, we are allowing those qualities to pass and to be passed. One visual tool we may utilize is the divine golden light that we may absorb together. It is 'darshan' for everybody, without need for superiority or position.

When we use this process, the healer enters a raised level of consciousness. He or she is temporarily dissolved from the world of matter and is able to absorb enough awareness of Love and Light to allow it to flow through to the one being healed, who we shall refer to as the healee.

Imagine then that we, being the healer, are brimming with Love and Light and that it overflows to the healee. The energy contact point is the third eye area, so the healer will look directly between the eyes and eyebrows of the healee.

Becoming filled with love and light, the healer may come to a point of actually seeing in gold, everything in their vision becoming golden. Then, a sphere of golden energy appears with a white-hot luminous center and we become aware that the sphere is moving, resonating with a musical accompaniment of two tones, the music of the spheres, as it were. This sphere may be between the healer and the healee at around head height.

We must hold that awareness for as long as it is comfortable for both parties. The healee may not see the sphere, or see gold, but the resonation of energy in the room will be of a high potency due to the vibrational presence of the spatial qualities.

Effects and results may include loss of awareness of time during the healing, the feeling of a true and profound spiritual experience, a sense of well-being, overwhelming feelings of peace and love. One day we will be able to pass this universal energy to each other automatically and humanity will evolve.

This process, like any process of healing, can only work if we create a circuit.

Spatial qualities represent the out flowing positive pole, the charge (+), the healer is the neutral (0) or conduit, and the healee is the receptive negative pole (-) receiving the charge. Once we share this awareness of energy we can understand that we have formed a relay or circuit within which the energy may begin, flow to and arrive.

Lovelight then, encapsulates *all* healing, it is totally inclusive of all forms, a spiritual aspect of being that we realize according to our awareness.

Chapter Ten:
ASPECTS OF BEING

Spiritual aspects of being occur when spatial abilities manifest in or flow through the individual. They become possible as we awaken more to consciousness, providing us with signposts to our potential.

When we absorb ourselves deeper into consciousness we are becoming increasingly aware of our true nature. As if we are a vessel being filled with the elixir of eternal life, we are able to experience those spiritual aspects that can only come around when we sense and touch upon the wholeness of our being. When we are filled, outlets naturally appear for these aspects of being to express themselves significantly in the lives of ourselves and others, benefiting all.

We can recognize examples of these aspects of being when we look back through our history.

"When we let freedom ring, when we let freedom ring from every village and every hamlet, from every state and every city, we will be able to speed up that day when all of God's children, black men and white men, Jews and Gentiles, Protestants and Catholics, will be able to join hands and sing in the words of the old Negro spiritual: Free at last! Free at last thank God almighty, we are free at last."

MARTIN LUTHER KING --WASHINGTON D.C - 28th AUGUST 1963.

The message in this quote clearly seeks unification and not the fracturation of humanity. The power and conviction with which it was delivered only helps us discern the truth of it.

Spiritual aspects of being are individual human expressions or manifestations that allow us to sense and share in the higher vibrations of love, truth and light, promoting a remembrance of our spiritual roots. They are individual in their realization but they constantly encourage unity.

The ability to transcend time and space provides an awareness that consciousness itself is eternal. How conscious we become in our lifetimes is defined by our ability to recognise and 'soak up' new vibrations as we awaken to their existence. The more aware we become, the greater clarity arises within us that we are more than just a body and the more truth we find in the realization that at some level in our being we are eternal.

We become connected to the stream of consciousness that gathers more and more water from the source. In doing so it seeks a multitude of ways to express itself as a whole.

We may realize that aspects of being (One) actually occur through cognizance, for the higher consciousness itself is not a commodity that comes and goes, it is purely our awareness of its existence which ebbs and flows.

What we may see as luck or misfortune can no longer be explained as coincidence or fate but assigned to the manifestation of our awareness. In realizing this, we move closer to the true beauty of our individual aspects of being.

INDIVIDUAL ASPECTS OF BEING: IS THAT NOT A FRACTIONATE STATE?

No. Aspects of being follow universal and spiritual laws and are only realized when we are seeking wholeness, not the dissolution of the awareness of One. For any group to be able to sustain its energy for the long term, it must have a common goal beneficial to all. Humanity's goals can only be decided by humanity. Looking at Europe for example, if common ground is based on beliefs common to all and unification of the whole, then it will last. If it is based on elements such as creation of more wealth and power for a few, then at some point it will fail, for it is not constructed on the wisdom of the perennial truths which consistently provide benefit for all.

Likewise, if we are to live together in peace and harmony in this world, we must seek the common source that binds all humanity.

When we become aware of the manifestation of aspects of our being, we no longer seek something, but become something, a part of a whole. We consciously become absorbed more profoundly into consciousness. Our stream has burst its banks and seeks to unify. When that water becomes a river it seeks other rivers, which in turn seeks to become unified into the form of an ocean.

The world and all that is in it, is approaching a time of radical movement. How that movement occurs will be the responsibility of all humanity.

We can choose to live our lives acquiring as much as we can for ourselves. We may seek contentment purely in the mind and the body; or we may seek the evolution of our human spirit, truly enabling progression.

Playing our part in the future of our world, the greatest role we may have as individuals is to seek to become One, to reach out for the One-ness. If you are not seeking, then you will, or you are about to, or you are in the process of doing so, for this is the very process of life itself. At any given moment it is our awareness of this that dictates how conscious we truly are.

Good and bad, love and hate, light and darkness, ignorance and truth – they are all opposites. But they are opposites in the poles of our being. If we can be one, we can become the other; the choice is a conscious one and comes down to our own free will.

What you chose you became, what you choose will be realized. But what are the consequences for yourself and others?

Proof is in the heart. Wherever we are on the path of life we can do no harm if we love one another as we love ourselves, for then we truly follow the heart that says: "We are all One."

CAN YOU EXPLAIN POLES OF BEING?

"Everything is dual; everything has poles; everything has its pair of opposites, like and unlike are the same; opposites are identical in nature, but different in degree; extremes meet; all truths are but half-truths; all paradoxes may be reconciled."

This is part of Hermetic Law, known to the oldest dynasties of Ancient Egypt. From this principle, we may see that hot is the opposite pole of cold, high the opposite of low and so on.

When we apply this to human existence, at one end we take the physical form of a body, and at the opposing pole, spirit. Our awareness of consciousness or spirit is what moves and transforms the reality of what we are. Good lies at the opposing pole of bad. But what is good to one may appear bad to another, for we are in the realms of the body and the mind, where one of us is right and the other one wrong. Poles are provided in order to allow discernment of individual truth.

The physical senses, the mind or the spirit discern what is good or bad. That is personal awareness. Through the connection of mind to spirit we transform ourselves by the increased absorption into the light of consciousness.

As our focus opens, our atoms move and change, manifesting in a transmutation of old characteristics and personality. No longer having the same interests, the same friends, the same perception, yet somehow knowing that we are all the time approaching truth, sensing the Path, are all proof that we are in a constant state of change and growth. When we like ourselves and others more and consciously move toward unifying one another, then we are moving away from our lower and into our higher nature, bringing significant changes that will reveal themselves in our aspects of being.

We may falter or fall at any point along the Path, but we will never go back. For we and the Universe are naturally expanding, constantly learning the art of expression.

We are living in order to die, dying in order to truly live.

There may be those amongst us who appear as if deaf to the whispers of change; but they are simply sitting there with their hands over their ears, unaware of their true selves at this point in time. Yet, when we are wholeheartedly embracing the truth of our spiritual nature, we are gaining a greater awareness, a truth that is eternal, that provides us with the sense that we are all One spirit, that the Source that we *all* came from has ONE mind, ONE body, ONE spirit.

In seeking what we seek, we may discover the reason why we seek. When we have what we sought, what we need to seek next will become clear; for nothing is new.

NOTHING IS NEW?

Anything or anybody who claims to be new, to hold the secret to success, to guarantee you health and happiness or untold wealth, fame and fortune, is that which is lower than your potential. For **your potential is in you**. And all these possibilities are provided in order that you may fulfil them in alignment with your choice of awareness. Any system of the human mind that seeks to dictate, seeks to control. Any system that acknowledges the concepts of superior and inferior can only provide balance when all becomes shared.

Fame is a short-lived thing when it is sought for itself, because what is its substance? It is just an illusion of success, a false impression of greatness, for that which is truly great is in ALL human beings – the courage of our struggle, the calm that arrives as if from nowhere in times of crisis, the understanding gained

from an illness, the experience of losing our loved ones, the joy at the birth of our children. Only when this journey is over do we recognize that the next leg of our travels has just begun and that our destination still remains somewhere far out in the greatness beyond.

Throughout time humanity has followed the wave of conscious growth (+), decline (-) and stagnation (0). The potential of the coming days is exciting for we are sensing a growth of human spirit and awareness unprecedented in our history. With the development of the Internet and the power of the media we are constructing bridges to old concepts with new possibilities. What those possibilities are, remains for us to (re)discover.

Release the burden of 'reality' and we will become the greatest number of explorers that have ventured this far.

By this we do not advocate losing the mind but rather using the mind in order to commit ourselves to change and transformation. Studying the inner stillness of the moment without accepting exterior distractions, allows us space to discern spiritual reality.

We can begin to sense that that which is just, is just for us all.

We can end that which is harming ourselves and others.

We can accept our bodies for what they are. For they will pass.

Realize those animalistic aspects of the mind as existing but controlled by our true selves.

In thought, word and deed, we can seek our highest potential and truest nature.

Share what good things we have with others, for it is theirs also.

Enjoy the success of others, for it is ours as well.

Acknowledge the presence of spirit in all things.

Remember those who came before us and those who will come after us, for we all need each other.

When sensing truth, accept it as one existing amongst many.

Plant the intention to make the world a better place for *all* humanity.

Inspire others by providing them with a reflection of themselves.

We can do all this, so that we may never forget that we are all One.

WE MAY CHOOSE TO EVOLVE, BUT WHAT IF OTHERS MAY NOT?

Then this is what needs to occur. We must never force or push our ideas on one another because in that fashion those ideas cannot be fully accepted. If those beliefs are driven into another's acceptance they will only provide an unstable base as a structure.

We cannot buy or sell spiritual truth; we can only find it.

We cannot share awareness with someone who does not have the same intention. Likewise, we would not sell water to an ocean yet we would give it to a thirsty man.

Chapter Eleven:
REPROGRAMMING THROUGH SOUL AND SPIRIT

If negative thoughts we wish to abate, we must concentrate on the opposite state.

In other words, when we discern that we are for example fearful, then we must install in ourselves the opposing thought or concept, which in this case is courage.

If we are truthful with ourselves, then we will be able to note either mentally or in writing those elements of our nature that we dislike or aspire to improve and transform. Only then can we work to silence those aspects by seeking their opposing nature. Once we can achieve this, we can look to move to allowing the lower instinctual behavior to be replaced by our higher nature.

You will recognise that you are a being of poles and that by applying one pole against another you will begin to change.

When we begin to dissolve our awareness and association with form and at the same time retain an awareness of it, then we can begin to reprogram ourselves by using spatial qualities to reach our highest potential.

Change ourselves for the better and we will inspire change in others.

The ability to transform or reprogram ourselves becomes an ongoing process according to our will. Effective reprogramming can impact all realms of our being, transforming body, mind and spirit.

CAN YOU DEFINE THE DIFFERENCE BETWEEN SPIRIT AND SOUL?

The soul is the individual mind presence that is personified energy. In life, everything we think, do or say, yields a distinctive energetic resonance. Your soul is the part of you that leaves the body behind at death, the result of the accumulated vibrations of your existence to date.

The spirit is the collective source of consciousness, the energy of the One-ness that our soul seeks to align itself with. Evolution is the process of coming from and returning to this source, for it is the Source of All being.

SO WE ARE SOUL?

This may be our cognizance, but in our fullest radiance and fusion with the Universe we are conscious that we are also spirit. Our evolution depends on growing out of the body, then out of the plane of soul and on to the 'lightest' or 'highest' vibrational state to join the stream of consciousness, to rejoin the Source.

Our soul holds the fundamental elements of consciousness, what we call mind and emotion. They are held in the electro-magnetic vacuum of the body until we pass from the physical plane of being. If we cannot shake off the concept of existing in a state separate to our body, we will remain energetically linked to the body; and at some future time we will be drawn back to the world of matter, to begin again.

When we pass over, we will still have choice. If we are unclear, the possibilities for our state of being will be unclear. But we may develop and recognize a sense of understanding the reality of this higher vibrational plane and of the process that we will all undergo one day. Gaining a deeper understanding of our mental / emotional balance and accumulating spatial qualities whilst physically alive will directly effect our passing over or transition to the next phase of our existence.

If we can begin to become aware that we are not purely a physical body while still living in one, then it will make the understanding of our new 'life' a lot easier when we don't have one anymore!

Our focus should turn away from 'things' and towards senses and feelings, so that we are able discern 'reality' when we are no longer surrounded by material objects. If we choose to recognize this now, today, then we will be consciously evolving the soul while still in a body.

When asking ourselves the purpose of this physical existence, we might not care, have no idea, or never have thought of it. We may be aware that the experience is showing us how to do it more efficiently next time. Perhaps our awareness of personal evolution revolves around the egoist states of perceived importance or success in our past or future incarnations. Maybe, just maybe, it is a fantastic opportunity to get to know our true selves, allowing the now.

Our free will dictates because we have choice. We have the possibility to discern. **We have the chance to truly find ourselves. If we do, we will find ALL of ourselves, for we are all One.**

We have so much potential, and yet we are still subject to the sometimes restricted workings of the mind. When we believe that we have choice, we can make a decision that makes the next part of our lives either complicated or trouble-free. This will be the result of our choice, subject to the laws of cause and effect.

The greater awareness of consciousness that we develop, the less opportunity the lower aspects of the mind of 'self' have to obstruct the expression of our spiritual growth. Of course, learning everything all over again is frustrating, but it is sometimes necessary.

We must learn to reprogram ourselves; for the program that was installed is way out of date and has been subjected to viruses and spam galore.

REPROGRAM OURSELVES?

That is exactly what we are doing by consciously evolving. But noticing that the things of *real* value have remained unchanged with the passing of time. Realizing that reprogramming is a genuine possibility allows us to become aware of our potential competence to self-transform. Undertaking reprogramming essentially allows more awareness, feeding our body and soul, disclosing our most significant aspects of being. Revealing all that we are to ourselves allows us to become.

This reality means no longer blaming your genes, your behavior, your personality, your body, or your intelligence on others. You are here, with freewill, to choose your future. Aligning the body to the resonance of the mind, and the mind to the higher vibrations of spirit creates a fully functional consciousness. From your original intention, you apply the focus of attention which provides the resulting vibration.

You are programmed by the codes of your D.N.A. But what controls D.N.A? You do. By knowing the possibility exists to alter the atomic state, you are responsible for your own reprogramming, for your thoughts, words and deeds. You can directly transform your being, because through the reprogramming of D.N.A., via the tool of consciousness, a significant reality will be recognized from the awareness of manifested spatial qualities. Therein lays the continuation of individual responsibility, no longer seeking to blame others for our weaknesses and problems, but rooting out the problems in order to prevent repetitive cycles of negativity.

We may learn this from the example of an illness, where a cure can only be realized by revealing and understanding the root cause. Taking cancer as one example; we discover that we have a growth. It is found by the doctors to be malignant. We decide to follow a prescribed treatment commencing with an operation to remove the growth, then a long period of radiation therapy followed by an even longer period of attempted recovery. But what was the cause of the lump in the first place? What allowed the cancer gene to attack the healthy cells? Science has proven the existence of the cancer gene, but what has given rise to the devastation of our healthy cells? The manifestation of any illness has occurred because the natural system of spirit to mind to body has been interrupted. Due to the mind's disconnection from spirit, it becomes over-burdened, and being unable to cope with the result, chaos ensues.

Establishing and treating the cause will prevent a repeat cycle of any illness.

SO ANY ILLNESS CAN BE REMEDIED?

Yes, when we are aware that this is the case. As some computer viruses may take more time to clear from the system than others, and anti-virus packages may only provide temporary relief, all 'infections' are removed by tracing the root of the problem, cleansing and returning the 'system' to complete functional being.

New illnesses will persist until we can understand how the harmonious balance of our threefold being creates our most efficient state. How each area of the body-mind-spirit in each person must be awakened and conditioned to allow whole being to manifest. For 'full' health can only be reached and maintained by awareness of all the parts contributing to whole being.

We may be aware that illness or dis-ease exists in order to teach ourselves the way to evolve; or we may see it as scientific fact.

What we may describe as "scientific fact" has climbed towards the top of the mountain, where consciousness has been sitting, waiting for her long awaited friend and equal, so that they could progress together, hand in hand, on the next leg of their journey.

Chapter Twelve:
THE METASENSES

As discussed before, nothing is really new. The properties and function of the atom were first theorised by Pythagoras, who later named it 'atoma.' His theories were developed by Democritus of Abdera, circa 400 B.C.E.; but it took us a while to evolve the full theory! So 'scientific fact' takes time to come to the awareness of the whole.

According to Democritus: "There are two forms of knowledge: one legitimate, one bastard. To the latter belong the following: sight, hearing, smell, taste, and touch. The legitimate is quite distinct from this. When the bastard form cannot see more minutely, nor hear, nor smell, nor taste, nor touch, then another finer form must be employed."

Science is realizing that what it considers to be new revolutionary discoveries are in fact age old theories and laws that are now being 'proven' by technology, only now becoming 'scientific fact.'

When we utilize our lowest abilities, we utilize our lowest senses.

Our highest senses are those which helpfully direct us on our path. How long this takes comes down to our awareness of those abilities that we cannot comprehend with our physical senses.

It is the higher or metasenses that provide us with our most efficient progress.

METASENSES?

Metaphysics is a branch of philosophy, brought through the awareness of Aristotle, who having completed his works on physics, sought the higher truths of the nature of reality and the place of humanity in the universe.

His " Ta meta ta physika biblia" detailed his philosophy on the existence of a higher form of physics. Having awareness of that which is above and beyond the physical senses is established by the use of what we call the higher or **metasenses.**

These senses allow us to discern spatial abilities, which in turn lead us to the embodiment of spatial qualities. Metasenses then are reflections of those senses that we have at the physical level, but of a higher finer vibration, which we may become aware of via the tool of consciousness.

With the use of the metasenses it is no longer the objective mind that denotes reason, but spatial consciousness itself that becomes the controlling aspect.

In this awareness, we 'feel' reality, and become aware of a finer form of underlying truth.

A metaphysician is somebody who seeks to understand those boundaries of existence that are currently unexplained by science. Both Plato and Einstein may be considered influential metaphysicians, who, linking the knowledge of the mind to the wisdom of consciousness, were able to throw new light upon existing thought, creating a new awareness of reality, via the weight of perception.

Using our metasenses, we are able to reason from a new position of awareness, as if we have been transformed from watching the sun come and go daily during our lives on Earth, to being able to see that the sun is always shining when we perceive it from deeper out in space. It is all a matter of perspective.

Extra-sensory perception is an evolution of the metasenses, and such skills as psychic awareness, mediumship, healing, channelling, remote viewing, auric vision, telepathy, telekinesis, altered states, automatic writing, inspired speech, are all examples of the individual growth in the evolution of our metasenses. Great poetry, great art and great music are those creative arts whereby we can still read, see or hear the traces of those metasenses developed throughout history, and the more these senses develop, the more we are able to receive from the positive interchange that occurs when contemplating, listening to, or reading them, for we may feel the existence of 'residual' energy, a reflection of the joy, the excitement, the rise in consciousness that was felt or perceived at the time of their creation.

But each of these skills or abilities that develop from the realization of our metasenses is not our final awareness, unless we choose it to be. Utilizing the metasenses relies on our ability to recognize the possibility that we can develop them in the first place, which in turn requires the actual experiencing of them in order that they can become 'planted' in our aspects of our being.

There are many roads that bring our awareness of the metasenses to the fore. It is possible that we study to be a good healer for years and years; and it is also possible that we discover that we can heal, and then seek to know more about that which we are.

Developing metasenses is not only a doorway into personal evolution, but for the progression of the whole species. Once experienced they cannot be denied, allowing all to receive some cognition of the stream of consciousness.

THE STREAM OF CONSCIOUSNESS?

The biologist and philosopher William James (1842-1910) used this phrase to describe the mind connection to the world. The school of modernist art and literature sprang from this awareness. He explained his awareness by suggesting that in order to evaluate what was the common good, we may need to incorporate "over-beliefs" for those things that we cannot experience. In general terms, we would need to keep an open mind to all things for those possibilities to potentially become reality. In this way, we can be aware that our thought of whatever we believe to be good can only be really proved to be reality by experiencing that goodness ourselves.

The stream of consciousness provides the sense of flow, and the feeling that we may become absorbed in it. But it also suggests that this stream has a source.

Allowing ourselves to be aware of the stream of consciousness may provide a realization that consciousness is not only within, but also without. It is manifest in everything. It is totally inclusive and not merely a tool for the gifted few.

For in a state of true awareness, consciousness is the underlying substance of all, the void between the atoms, the invisible One-ness, the very spirit of God.

*

Our understanding of complete reality may be similar to that of a little fish living at the bottom of a huge ocean, who understands what is real by instinct and by copying the ways of the other fish. He knows how to move, swim, feed, mate, and so on. One day, on his travels, he decides to explore the higher parts of his world. He eventually reaches the surface, and basks in the warmth of something he hasn't seen or felt before, all the same, it feels good. All of a sudden, a huge seagull swoops down and takes him. They fly upwards and he can't believe the feelings he can sense, in a world he never knew existed. The seagull accidentally lets go of the slippery fish, who falls back into the water, where he swims quicker than ever before in his attempts to reach home. Back at the bottom of the reef, he excitedly tells his family and friends of his bizarre experience. They look at him in disbelief; it wasn't true they said, he must have imagined it, after all they had never heard of such a ridiculous thing. The confused little fish takes his place at the bottom of the reef once more, but he knows what really happened, he can't forget. The next day he goes back again, and the next day, and the next day, until one day he doesn't come back home at all.

*

So our world becomes defined by the parameters of our experience, for it is that which we comprehend as 'reality.' When we begin to develop the metasenses, we are leaving the world of material 'reality,' and beginning to perceive another finer form of 'reality.'

Like truth, one perceived reality is only a part reality of the whole.

Even those who are not directly aware of experiencing the reality of the metasenses are now coming around to the common consensus that although they may not have experienced them, their existence is in fact a distinct rational possibility, for this is the weight of perception in action.

The next phase of that awareness for those who sense this, is preparing themselves to move into it. If we are not conscious that we are seeking to evolve our awareness, we are not unconscious, but we cannot guarantee that events will not overtake us, and force a release into a higher consciousness.

This is what happens with the tragic world events that occur on a regular basis, for as the weight of perception of consciousness builds; there arise compensatory cataclysmic reactions in the physical world. We may see this manifest as a financial collapse of the world markets, a terrorist attack, a war, or devastation from tsunamis, earthquakes and the like. As we dive headfirst into physical and mental chaos, the spiritual consciousness recompenses us. As the two opposing poles of spirit and matter swing to and fro they produce reactions to each other which manifest in the world.

We can see this occur in life when we experience the loss of a loved one. On learning of the death of someone close, we enter various negative states that interconnect between shock, grief, disbelief, confusion, guilt and anger. If we eventually come to terms with the physical loss, we can move into a different awareness of acceptance. From there, we can perceive that **death is just a part of the wonderful experience of life** and that we will ALWAYS remember the beautiful positive experiences of love and joy that we shared with our loved one. Those memories become timeless and eternal, for they are ever present energetic vibrations.

Being conscious of the polarities that exist in all aspects of life we may see that all is interlinked; the state of the whole is the pivotal control of the overall manifestation of the parts. We have a responsibility to each other to evolve the whole; otherwise, we will continue to experience great adversity in this world.

This brings to mind a quote by Maurice Barbanell: "The simple truth is that God has made us all of one spirit.

Whether we like it or not, the universal laws have so ordained it that the cannibal, the Negro, the Red Indian, the Aborigine and the members of every race, irrespective of the color of their skins, are spiritual kith and kin. Spiritually, we are members of one another, all children in the divine family. This is, in fact, the Spiritual United Nations."

Let's not wait for the world to change;
let's change the world.

We can begin today, this very minute, because we are all human beings and not one of us is perfect, for perfection and matter are incompatible.

SOME SAY THAT PERFECTION HAS LIVED ON THIS EARTH BEFORE.

That would be their awareness at this time, and we respect all awareness.

If that helps them to create a process of unification and not fractionation, then that is all well and good. If however, it creates another hierarchy of difference, and teaches mankind that they are flawed, guilty sinners, ripe for punishment, or that one race is special or chosen above others, then that is another matter. Any religious school of thought that indicates their truth as being absolute or the use of fear as a technique of control is fatally flawed. Any teacher who purports to be a spiritual teacher and to know more than you is spiritually lacking. Any system of faith that pertains to have uniqueness in any shape or form at the base of their foundation is flawed. If it is the first this, or the last that, it is flawed.

If it is a part of the whole, a truth of many truths, with a doctrine of love and not fear, then it is a greater manifestation of spirit than others not endowed with the same qualities.

We may have an awareness of the 'God consciousness' of any religious institution by the criteria it is founded upon, as well as by seeing to what extent the institution has the ability to develop or transform the spiritual nature. If we follow that course, then we will eventually gain more ground on the mountain of truth, through having an awareness of what is wrong, rather than continuously disagreeing because we were taught that our faith holds the unique rights to truth.

Religion without science is as dangerous as science without religion.

Now that we are seeing the two being drawn closer and closer, we can look forward with great excitement over the coming years. Science has already proven what the philosophers of Ancient Egypt knew fully well, that **matter is an illusion or a representation of our experience of consciousness.**

A recent example of the blending of science and spirit is the employment of sensitives (those who have recognized use of the metasenses) by commercial industry. The computer and mobile phone watchdogs have recognized a link between sensitives feeling unwell, and their exposure to the radiation that is emitted from masts and mini dishes. It has become a recognized condition in open minded countries, such as Sweden, where the link has been proven by their own scientists. The Swedish government estimates that around 3% of the population is what they call electro hyper sensitive. We would be aware that if these figures were correct, then around 3% of the population has, whether they are aware of it or not, begun development of the metasenses.

When we experience the metasenses in action, we can begin to comprehend the greater reality. If we go beyond that and question the why and how, we gain ground in our individual and unitary evolution.

We begin to see that we are all One, not just humanity, but nature, the Universe, and all the many life forms that exist. All are One.

Spiritually, we are the microcosm, because everything follows the same universal laws and degrees. The Ancient Greeks seeking the reason for existence, realized that the same traits that occur in one human being occur in the entire population, and philosophised that it was the same in nature, and indeed the whole universe, that a connection existed that was common and binding to all the parts.

Further back still, the hermetic axiom of "As above, so below," gave the earliest Ancient Egyptians the awareness that all that exists in the entirety of the Cosmos is mirrored in the human being, the smaller universe. The application of this awareness reveals the repetition of pattern and form to those things that appear chaotic or irrational to our normal objective understanding. Indeed it is an important part of coming to understand how Hermetic laws or principles may be understood to apply to every plane of existence.

CAN YOU TELL US MORE ABOUT HERMETIC LAWS?

There are many publications that deal with these philosophic principles, and through applying the Hermetic principles or concepts, we can learn to understand the spiritual science that lies behind transformation, or transmutation.

Below is a brief summary of the Hermetic principles;

- Mentalism: True reality is spirit, and the ALL is pure spirit.
- Correspondence: "As above, so below." All planes of existence correspond and reflect each other.
- Vibration: Everything, including body, mind and spirit, is in a constant state of movement. This vibration exists at varying rates, from matter on upwards, the lighter and finer the vibration, the higher the position in the scale.
- Polarity: Everything is dual. Everything has its pair of opposites.
- Rhythm: Everything flows in and out. Everything has its tides.
- Cause and Effect: Every cause has an effect and every effect a cause.
- Gender: Everything has masculine and feminine principles. Gender manifests itself on all planes.

The principle of mentalism is the kingpin of transformative change. Having discerned the three interlinked areas of human consciousness that together make up the whole, we can learn to comprehend the realities revealed by our metasenses.

Closer to today, Aldous Huxley (1894 – 1963) who was a writer, author and philosopher, and one of the most gifted academic intellects of recent times, was compelled in 1945, (as was Ghandi with his "Many Paths, One Universe"), to compile a philosophy that set about unifying what he saw as universal truths and values common to all humanity. Huxley's book was entitled "The Perennial Philosophy".

These are some of the main conclusions:

- That physical existence is only one plane of reality; non-physical realities exist. The material world is the shadow of a higher reality which cannot be brought to reason by the normal senses, but that human spirit bears testimony to it.
- Physical existence in the form of the body is subject to physical laws of decay. The higher

aspect of our existence is not subject to decay, but to eternal spiritual laws. This has been greatly ignored in the West.
- ALL humans have a capacity to discern the nature of reality and the ultimate truth. That seeking these is the purpose of our existence. All religions have an absolute principle, either named or formless, a God or a state, from which all existence originated, and to which all existence will eventually return.

"The last end of every human being (is) ... to find out who he really is. "A. Huxley

Summation

CONCLUSIONS GAINED FROM THE APPLICATION OF THE SPIRITUAL PRINCIPLE "WE ARE ALL ONE":

The longing for spiritual communion exists in all human beings. We may achieve this coming together by learning to expand our field of consciousness, thus raising our vibration to enable the development of spatial qualities.

In order to most efficiently or consciously evolve, we need to manifest these spatial qualities in a constructive way that may bring about transformation to ourselves and others, the environment that we inhabit and the world that we live in.

The fundamental reward of life may be realized by spiritual or conscious evolution, absorbing the higher resonances of consciousness. This is the point of existence, to evolve, thereby inspiring growth in others.

With the present state of the world, we are beginning to ride the tidal wave of change, part of which we will see over the next few years, but particularly the portal for change in 2012.

These times allow for the possibility of a new dawn, a golden age in the history of mankind; but this will only come to fruition when we take individual responsibility, which in turn will progress the whole.

Our spiritual evolution will decide how and when this new dawn may occur, but unification is inevitable, one way or another.

2012 remains an actual state of consciousness that will manifest correspondingly to the 'weight of perception' of all humanity.

When we look back through the history of our world, we can trace the evolutionary chain back to its origins deep in space, for that is where we come from. Our spiritual aspects are essentially 'alien' to our bodies. The true essence of our being is not matter but energy, and we should understand that whatever denies or stands in the way of the evolving consciousness becomes redundant or overtaken.

We need not continue the dysfunctional existence in ignorance of our whole state of being, for we may realize that we rely too much on what we see and not enough on what we feel.

Becoming consciously evolved can only occur when we realize that spirit is the source of our being. That all sprang forth from the One primordial particle. We are all of one spirit, so we all have the same spiritual abilities and capacities, all have the same potential to develop spatial consciousness and therefore spatial qualities. We also have the ability to shape our aspects of being into a force that is a positive addition to the whole.

The bodies we inhabit are not the final stage of evolution, but a phase of growth that will continue until one day future generations may turn back the pages of history to read of these times, of all that occurred in the period of 2008-2012 and be honored to be the advanced beings that evolved from us.

We need not fear death, but instead seek to understand it. When we pass over to the other side, we may compare it to passing out, losing consciousness of this physical world, at the same time becoming more conscious of the continued existence of our soul.

There is a plane of soul where we may continue to learn more of the essence of spirit, becoming yet more conscious. In the soul-state, the previously accumulated vibrations of our physical lives initially dictate our presence.

Evolution of the soul continues by the seeking of alignment with the Source of creation. For this to happen, we will arrive at a stage of the dissolution of our form, in order that our soul may join with the One-ness of all Being.

The opportunity that we have now is to align soul and spirit, via the expansion of our field or awareness of consciousness, thus allowing a physical manifestation, a quickening of the evolutionary process.

The key to evolution is conscious spiritual transformation. This medium allows positive change in the individual and the whole.

All 'truths' are only part 'truths.' As we develop spiritually, we may learn to discern the truth required for the continuation of growth.

We all travel a path, whether we have an awareness of it or not. It is a road of mistakes and opportunities, one that we must individually follow to enable our evolution to be free of the restriction of the minds of others.

We must learn from our significant experiences. These are the truly transformational opportunities that present us with a window of potential.

Everything is conscious to a degree. The wonderful opportunity that we have as human beings is the expansion of our consciousness. We are the most evolved being on planet Earth and we must all take responsibility as such, making conscious efforts to seek unity using all the means we have available.

The 'awareness of One' can be a useful tool to hold our awareness of spiritual equality. The end result of our combined efforts will come about through the principle of the 'weight of perception.'

Illness exists in the lower vibrations of mind and body, not in our spirit, the source of the cure. The vibrational resonance of our spirit does not allow for the attachment of the lower energy of the mind and body. We choose to be ill, and choose not to become ill; just as we may choose to die or not to die.

We will solve many problems in our world if we learn to deal with the root cause of problems, rather than treating the symptoms. For example, when we seek to end devastation in a third world country, we should firstly seek the cause of that devastation and then we will be able to provide a permanent long term solution. If we do not seek the root of the problem, we will fall back into a repetitive cycle of ignorance, and in doing so resolve nothing.

We are never alone unless we choose to be alone. We must accept the variety of ups and downs that life provides in abundance, remembering that every experience has a reason and seek to find its purpose or meaning. Again, all things have a reason for there is reason in all things. All things must pass.

Contemplating one another's perceived faults leads us to spiritual stagnation; yet, recognizing another's qualities is transformational.

When we harness the principle of focusing our attention, we are aware that we become our focus. That which is constant in our mind is that which creates our manifested state of vibration.

Colors, numbers, symbols and names all have significant spiritual meanings and it is for the individual to recognize these as stages according to their own awareness.

Spatial qualities may be manifested in a receptive person or pole of charge, which in turn provides inspiration to others.

The more aware we become, the more we receive from interaction in our daily lives. Only then may we come to realize the power of 'positive interchange,' which is the giving or receiving of higher consciousness that results in positive growth.

Nothing is really new, because the cycle of creation

comes from the Source to a point of release to the whole and therefore the concept of originality or ownership is a misconception of the mind of 'self,' and not relative to our spiritual nature.

We can never really 'have' or own anything apart from the freedom of choice. How we use that depends upon our awareness and our focus.

Perceived 'reality' is only limited by the vibrational state of the mind, which comes about by our individual balance of body, mind and spirit as it becomes manifested in our 'state of being.'

There are three parts to every human being, the lowest state of vibration being the body, because it manifests as matter, the middle part being the individual mind or soul, and finally the connection to the unified state of spirit, which we are inseparable from, yet not always conscious of.

Reprogramming our atomic structure and altering our D.N.A. is a reality because of consciousness. When we understand the full consequences of that, we may comprehend our direct, active role in the evolution of the human race.

Metasenses are those higher senses that we may accumulate with our gradual absorption to greater consciousness. Through the development of these metasenses we may learn to transcend this 'reality' and to manifest spatial, 'divine' transformational qualities.

Tools of reflection such as the Hermetic principles allow us to stay on the path of belief and awareness that exists alongside human evolution. These are perennial truths. They were true in the past, are true in the present, and will continue to be true in the future, when we will have a greater understanding of their implications.

They remain unblemished by time, for their existence is the result of our combined awareness to the spiritual reality:

¤ WE ARE ALL ONE ¤

Dubon

The 'Dubon Centre of Healing and Awareness' was founded by Jonathan and Wendy Harrison, along with fellow truth-seeker Sharon Jeffries.

Set in twenty-six acres of rural Gascony, 'Dubon' has been lovingly restored to provide comfortable accommodation in an idyllic, peaceful setting.

Visitors to 'Dubon' are offered the opportunity to share in a limited number of tailor-made visits incorporating the conscious evolution of 'We Are All One'. Working as a team and concentrating on your mind – body – spirit needs, we ensure you gain the utmost from your stay.

If you would like to visit 'Dubon' please email us and we'll do our very best to accommodate you.

Subject to demand and availability, we also take part in

associated events, workshops and seminars outside of the centre.

Please be sure to contact us well in advance to avoid disappointment.

    Email: dubon@neuf.fr
    Web: www.dubon.org

Made in the USA